the Knitchic
GUIDE
TO
SWEATERS

Marcelle Karp &
Pauline Wall

Classic styles for the modern knitter

NORTH LIGHT BOOKS
Cincinnati, Ohio

www.mycraftivity.com

The Knitchicks' Guide to Sweaters. Copyright © 2009 by Marcelle Karp and Pauline Wall. Manufactured in China. All rights reserved. The written instructions, photographs, designs, patterns and projects in this volume are intended for the personal use of the reader and may be reproduced for that purpose only. Any other use, especially commercial use, is forbidden under law without the express written permission of the copyright holder. Violators will be prosecuted to the fullest extent of the law. No other part of this book may be reproduced in any form or by any electronic or mechanical means including information storage and retrieval systems without permission in writing from the publisher, except by a reviewer, who may quote a brief passage in review. Published by North Light Books, an imprint of F+W Media, 4700 East Galbraith Road, Cincinnati, Ohio 45236. (800) 289-0963. First edition.

13 12 11 10 09   5 4 3 2 1

Distributed in Canada by Fraser Direct
100 Armstrong Avenue
Georgetown, ON, Canada L7G 5S4
Tel: (905) 877-4411

Distributed in the U.K. and Europe by David &
Charles
Brunel House, Newton Abbot, Devon, TQ12 4PU,
England
Tel: (+44) 1626 323200, Fax: (+44) 1626 323319
E-mail: postmaster@davidandcharles.co.uk

Distributed in Australia by Capricorn Link
P.O. Box 704, S. Windsor, NSW 2756 Australia
Tel: (02) 4577-3555
Library of Congress Cataloging-in-Publication
Data

Karp, Marcelle.
    The knitchicks' guide to sweaters : classic styles
for the modern knitter / Marcelle Karp and Pauline Wall.
        p. cm.
    Includes index.
    ISBN 978-1-60061-096-7 (softcover : alk. paper)
  1. Knitting. 2. Knitting--Patterns. 3. Sweaters.
I. Wall, Pauline. II. Title.
    TT825.K39 2009
    746.43'2041--dc22
                            2008047028

Metric Conversion Chart

to convert	to	multiply by
Inches	Centimeters	2.54
Centimeters	Inches	0.4
Feet	Centimeters	30.5
Centimeters	Feet	0.03
Yards	Meters	0.9
Meters	Yards	1.1
Sq. Inches	Sq. Centimeters	6.45
Sq. Centimeters	Sq. Inches	0.16
Sq. Feet	Sq. Meters	0.09
Sq. Meters	Sq. Feet	10.8
Sq. Yards	Sq. Meters	0.8
Sq. Meters	Sq. Yards	1.2
Pounds	Kilograms	0.45
Kilograms	Pounds	2.2
Ounces	Grams	28.3
Grams	Ounces	0.035

Editor: Jessica Gordon

Designer: Marissa Bowers

Layout Designer: Kelly O'Dell

Production Coordinator: Greg Nock

Photographer: Stephen Murello

Stylist: Abby Jenkins

Technical Editor: Alexandra Virgiel

www.fwmedia.com

Dedications

Marcelle
For my daughter Ruby and my mother Shula.

Pauline
For Natasha Dean.

Acknowledgments

Marcelle
I would like to thank...

Pauline, for her partnership; Maren Waxenberg, for her insight on steeking and for showing me how to be the parent I am; Kendrick, for inspiring me to make him the gorgeous sweater he wears so proudly; Wendy, who I miss every day.

I'd also like to thank Anne-So, Elise, Kristin, Mikki, Sia, Josh, Matty, Olivier, Paul. And my family: Mom, Dad, Jerry, Rose. And Ruby. Always Ruby.

From Both of Us
We would like to thank our literary agent, Andrea Somberg, for being a tremendous champion of our work. Thanks as well to our editor, Jessica Gordon, for her infinite patience. Finally, thanks to our photographer, Stephen Murello, for his generous talent.

Pauline
I would like to thank...

Marcelle, who inspired me to pick up my sticks in the first place; Zenia, who introduced us; Helen, Melanie and Loba, knitters and organizers extraordinaire, who inspired and motivated me, providing friendship and endless cups of tea.

I would also like to give big love and thanks to the knitters and crafty lasses in my life: Ting, Emma and Rachel (for patient test knitting), Gail, Lucy, Lotta, Olivia, Claire, Adrienne, Jenny, Rachel, Betsy, Claire, Kate, Shirley, the lovely ladies at Liberty, and the cabal of online knitters and friends.

Thank you also to Emerald Mosley for the Knitchicks Web site design.

Most importantly, I would like to thank Fred for his support and Rosie for keeping my yarn warm.

Contents

THE KNITCHICKS' STORY 6

KNITSTORY: A LITTLE BACKGROUND ON THE HISTORY OF KNITTING 8

KNITCHICKS' GEAR 10

KNITCHICKS' BASICS: TECHNIQUES 16

In the Beginning...The First Stitch 17

The Middle...Knitting and Purling 24

The Shape of Things to Come... Increasing and Decreasing 28

The End...Binding Off and Seaming Up 31

YOU SAY JUMPER, I SAY SWEATER: LEARNING THE BASICS OF SWEATER KNITTING 34

ME! ME! ME! 40
Patterns for Women

Shula 42

Jess 46

Allez Hélène 50

Isla 54

Marcelle 58

Morgan 62

Mini Morgan 66

Loba 70

Pam 74

Raven 78

Thelma & Louise 82

Summer 84

Moni 88

Layla 92

LITTLE DARLINGS 96
Patterns for Babies and Kids

Baby Diamond 98

Jarrah 100

Kaia 102

Oscar 108

Ruby Ruffle 112

Ruby's Cami 116

Ruby's Shrug 120

Aviva 122

Aviva Redux: The Dress 124

OKAY, OKAY, HIM TOO 126
Patterns for Men

Kendrick 128

Your Boyfriend's Jumper 132

Michael 136

ABBREVIATIONS 140

RESOURCES 140

FURTHER READING 141

INDEX 142

MARCELLE

PAULINE

The Knitchicks' Story

Marcelle

Crafts have long been woven into the intricate fabric of my family's life. As a young girl, I watched my mother sew costumes, hem pants and create full wardrobes for me and my brother with her green iron Singer sewing machine. My mom was an infallible craft goddess to me, seamlessly spinning her own fashionista's doctrine; I wanted to make things just like she did.

As soon as my fingers could work a needle or two, Mom taught me to knit and crochet, although the sewing machine was hands-off until I was in my teens. I crocheted yarmulkes for boys I liked (the yeshiva girl equivalent of mixed tapes), and Mom and I would sit on the couch on Friday nights, watching *Dallas* and knitting, side by side.

For my mother, making garments by hand wasn't a feminist statement—it was her creative outlet, a natural part of the new girl order for many generations of the women on my mother's side of the family. I hold my mother's legacy in my hands now as I sew bags, knit dresses and crochet rock star scarves for my daughter Ruby, who wears it all proudly and with the fierce, feisty attitude of a true feminist fashionista.

For many years, I was crafting on my own—in my apartment, in cafes, while traveling. The bubble burst for me in the early '90s when *BUST*, the magazine I co-created with Debbie Stoller (yes, the *Stitch 'n Bitch* maven), started our DIY column, "She's Crafty." The column embraced what was once known as woman's work as part of our feminist discourse. Craft enthusiasts have come a long way since the days of my mother's Singer machine. Creativity has flourished in the public arena, and we have long since stopped knitting behind closed doors, preferring to share our work in books and magazines, online and in knitting circles. It's a good time to be crafty.

Pauline

My first introduction to knitting was in school, where we had been forced to learn to knit—our first project was baby booties, no less. What kid wants to make baby booties? I convinced a friend to knit mine while I sat and chatted in the back of the classroom. From that point on, I had no interest in the craft at all, so I was surprised to see how much my friend Marcelle enjoyed it when she visited me in Australia with her baby. She knitted like a machine, and, shockingly, she even seemed to enjoy it.

My curiosity was piqued, but the final motivation to pick up yarn and needles didn't come until I was serving jury duty some months after Marcelle's visit. My fellow jurors and I were often sent out of the courtroom while "points of law" were discussed. Sitting in a room with complete strangers was uncomfortable—I didn't feel relaxed enough to read a book, and, of course, no television was allowed. My mind wandered back to Marcelle and her devotion to her craft. I couldn't see the attraction, but I trusted her judgment. Equipped with some purple kids' yarn, 4.5mm needles and a book, I settled in to reteach myself to knit. The other jurors were fascinated, and suddenly we had something to talk about. Between the twelve of us we managed to work out how to cast on and remembered the knit stitch. Everyone had a go, and by the end of the case we had half an ugly, misshapen purple scarf.

After that, I was hooked. I joined a knitting circle, a rather motley group that met often in each other's living rooms to drink tea, eat cake and craft. We embroidered, tapestried, glitter-glued cardboard and called it a picture frame, and, above all, we knit.

Then I moved from Australia to London, and I found myself knitting alone. I was really missing my crafty chicas back home. I thought, surely in such a big city there must be more people who want to knit. But how was I to find them? I had been blogging for a year, so I really already knew the answer: I would go online. I created a small site with a single posting, and two people showed up to that first group (turns out, they were the greatest two people I could have hoped to meet and are now firm friends). Eventually, the community grew. Now Knitchicks is the resource for knitters in the United Kingdom to find each other. We even launched Knitchicks events, including groups in Canary Wharf at lunchtime and in the city of London after work to cater to London's diverse population. We also briefly held "Knitflicks: Knitting in the Cinema," a monthly event where we watched a new release with the house lights on (first rule of Knitflicks: no subtitles). Once we even had an Afternoon Tea Circle Line party, where we met at a designated subway station and boarded the train with knitting projects in hand.

Join the Knitchicks Circle

Many friendships, as well as knitting know-how, form in the comfort of the knitting circle. With this book in your hand, you are now part of the Knitchicks, an ever-growing knitters' circle. Wherever you are, you are always a Knitchick (even if you're a boy!). Visit www.knitchicks.co.uk, start a blog and kick off a Knitchicks gang.

What does being a Knitchick mean? It means you're interested in the craft of knitting, maybe even crocheting. It means you are constantly learning about the craft and you are interested in expanding and sharing what you know with who you know. It means you are embracing your own style, adding your special touch as you learn more and more, whether you are following a pattern to the letter or adding to it. Every crafty person has their own style; no matter what your skill level, you have a personal touch that you bring to every project—from your tension to your color choices to the way you bind off! So go on, make your mark and show us—and, more importantly, show yourself—what you can do.

Knitstory

A Little Background on the History of Knitting

It's not easy to work out who invented knitting or when it began, but it looks like it all started with the humble sock.

Socks dating back to the third century CE have been found in Egypt. These early socks were constructed using a method called, for obvious reasons, "single-needle knitting."

Single-needle knitting (also known as nålebinding or naalbinding) is a technique of linking loops to one another using a needle and thread/yarn that is pulled in its entirety through each loop. For this technique to work, the yarn cannot be too long, and it seems additional pieces were spliced together (or perhaps woven in). These socks were worked from the toe up, and they stopped just under the ankle. Coptic or Romano-Egyptian socks dating back to around 5 CE have a separate toe, like Japanese tabi socks. We can take this as evidence that the sock-and-sandal-wearing fashion has a long history!

Although the first examples of single-needle knitting were found in Egypt, the Vikings were the ones to spread the nålebinding (the word itself being Danish) technique to western Europe. The "Coppergate sock" found in York dates back to 10 CE and is assumed to be the result of Viking influence.

Somewhere between this time and the thirteenth century, knitting as we know it developed. Islamic socks with rich colors and beautiful patterns (including the words for "God" and "blessings") were found in Egypt. A cushion from northern Spain dating to around 1275 (finally something other than socks!) was knitted in a fine-gauge stocking stitch with (among other things) *fleur-de-lys* patterns and Islamic blessings. This cushion was found in the grave of a Christian prince buried in a monastery; this suggests that knitting was introduced into Europe by Arabs through the Iberian Peninsula.

The next significant knitting references we have are paintings of the Madonna knitting, the first by Lorenzetti in northern Italy from circa 1345 (*Madonna dell'umilita*) and the more famous one by Master Bertram of Minden in Buxtehude (near Hamburg in northern Germany), among others. The significant detail to note about these paintings is that the Madonna is knitting in the round on four needles!

Circular knitting was all the rage for a long time. In fact, evidence suggests that the purl stitch was invented in the late sixteenth century. By this time, knitted socks and undergarments were popular among Europe's wealthiest citizens. Everyone was knitting stockings in England, and by the end of the sixteenth century, they were the leading producer of stockings.

William Lee invented (and refined) the knitting frame in the late sixteenth century. At the time, his invention was met with little enthusiasm. The product was considered coarse and the process slow. Although hardly popular, The Framework Knitters' Company was established in 1657. It was a hundred years before the speed of frame knitting posed a threat to hand knitting—at first, frame knitting was slow to adapt to fashion changes and required daylight, so handknitting was more practical. During this time, hand-knitting for profit was done by the poor, and especially children, often to supplement the family income.

Over the following two hundred years, the knitting cottage industry was killed off by the industrial revolution. By the mid-nineteenth century, knitting arrived in parlors as a leisure activity for ladies. Ganseys and jerseys were knit in the homes of (and by) fishermen.

The twentieth century was a roller coaster of knitting activity. The First World War encouraged a flurry of knitting for the troops: Socks, mitts and helmet liners were industriously created for the soldiers by those at home. The enthusiasm for knitting did not wane after the war, and during the 1920s knitting became high fashion. The Parisian houses all produced wonderful designs, most famously Elsa Schiaparelli's *trompe l'oeil* bow. The ensuing Second World War and the associated austerity of that time again made knitting a necessity.

In more recent decades, cheap labor sources in Asia and emerging synthetic fibers have firmly ended the "Make Do and Mend" mentality. Inexpensive knitwear is now readily available, and knitting has once again become a pasttime rather than a necessity. Until very recently, handknitting has been associated with members of the older generation who remember the shortages of war time and choose to inflict ghastly creations on defenseless grandchildren!

This brings us up to the reemergence of knitting as a hobby in the early twenty-first century. This surge in popularity is most probably a result of the Internet, which introduced new ways to share techniques and patterns as well as created a new marketplace for yarns. Online communities have brought together enthusiasts from around the world and from varied socioeconomic statuses to once again embrace this noble craft.

And 1,500 years later, we're still knitting socks.

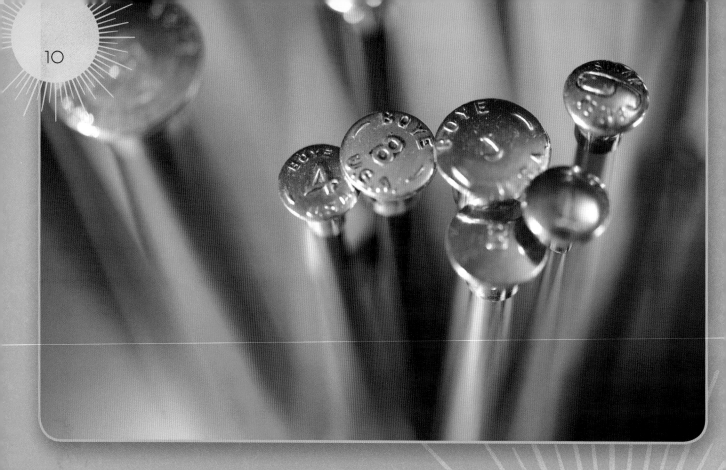

Knitchicks' Gear

How did our ancestors (and our moms!) make do with only a few aluminum needles and a tape measure? Today, Knitchicks seem to need more tchotchkes than ever to knit. We need crochet hooks and tapestry needles and bobbins and a separate wing for storing it all. In this chapter, we talk about the basics—what you really do need—as well as the fun stuff that you can collect if you want. For instance, you can put your notions in a sassy pouch the size of a make-up bag instead of letting them run rampant at the bottom of your backpack. You can light a Knit-a-row-matherapy candle to burn in the background while you work on your *Aviva* jumper (see page 122). You can even use your collection of shot glasses to store your stitch markers!

Helpful Hint

As you start to amass a knitting needle collection, you'll want to figure out where to store them. We suggest you use everyday household items!

For Circulars: Place same-size needles in zippered plastic bags and label them.

For Straight and Double-Pointed: Use a vase. Your needles will look like bare willow branches.

Tools of the Trade: Needles

Just like knitters themselves, needles come in all shapes and sizes, from tiny double-pointed needles to thick, shiny circulars. With knitting needles, as with so many aspects of the knitter's world, size matters. Why? Choosing the correct combination of needles and yarn is essential for creating the type of knitted fabric you want. Your choices may also be driven by your comfort zone. For instance, Marcelle can't knit on size 2 needles, while Pauline handles them like a pro. Marcelle's penchant for larger needles drives her to choose thicker yarns, while Pauline is quite comfortable picking skinny yarns. It's all a matter of what size feels right.

Needles in the Know

Knitting needles are manufactured from all sorts of materials. Try out a few pairs to see what you like best. You may also find that some needles go better with certain types of fibers than others. For example, super-smooth needles plus super-smooth yarn equals slippery stitches that slide easily from needle to needle (this is great if you're an experienced knitter with a yen for speed...but not so great if you're a green beginner). And squeaky acrylic on grabby bamboo may lead to stubborn stitches that refuse to slide along the needles (stitches with staying power may be great for socks or for beginners who need help keeping the stitches from falling off the needles...but they're rather annoying for veteran knitters who want to knit fast).

Needle tips also come in different shapes. Wood and bamboo needle tips tend to be stubby, while metal needles often have more streamlined tips. The pointiest of all needles are those made for lace knitting, although they can be used for any project. Following are descriptions of the most common needle materials.

Aluminum (nickel and nickel-plated): These needles are turbo charged! Yarn glides along the metal so smoothly and quickly that many people call these the fastest needles around.

Bamboo: Always dependable, bamboo needles are light and a bit flexible. Bamboo is a sustainable resource, so it's probably the most environmentally conscious choice.

Casein: These needles are made of organic materials. Casein is a protein made of milk. Go green!

Glass: Clear or brightly colored, these needles are functional works of art—wicked cool to knit with and surprisingly strong.

Plastic: These needles are the most economical choice, and they're good for learning. Bryspun brand plastic needles are recommended for knitters with arthritis. Watch out—plastic needles can snap more easily than needles made from other materials.

Wood: Beautiful and smooth, wood needles are a real treat! Wood needles are often made of birch, ebony or rosewood, but they can also be cherry, maple or walnut.

Needles Are Us

Different knitting projects require different types of needles. The three basic kinds of needles are straight, circular and double-pointed. Each type of needle is suited to a particular type of knitting. Choose what works best for you.

Straight: The most iconic knitting implement, these needles come as a matching pair of two straight sticks in varying lengths with a flattened knob at one end to stop the knitting from sliding off.

Circular: The real workhorse of handknitting, circular needles are two needle tips connected by a flexible cord generally made of nylon. Use circular needles to knit in the round or to knit large projects back and forth so the weight of the knitting rests in your lap instead of being supported by your wrists. You can purchase circular needles in interchangeable sets that allow you to create whatever size needle you want connected with whatever length of cord you desire. Very considerate, these are.

Double-Pointed: You can work these shorter sticks in multiples, like a puppeteer! Double-pointed needles come in a set of four or five, and they're used to knit small pieces in the round, such as sleeves, socks or the tops of hats.

Size Me Up

Needles come in all different lengths and thicknesses. This can get confusing because there are generally three numbers attached to size, all of which generally appear on the needle.

Diameter: A needle's diameter is measured in millimeters. The US size is given as a corresponding number.

Shaft: How long is this needle anyway? The length of the needle is usually given on the needle packaging. For circular needles, the length is measured from tip to tip and includes the joining cord.

Helpful Hint

The smaller the diameter of the needle, the thinner the yarn you should pair with the needles. The larger the diameter, the thicker the yarn. If you have a yarn you want to manipulate a bit, you can experiment by going up or down one or two diameter sizes to see how the fabric changes.

The Needle Size Chart

Knitters work a great deal with charts. Here is one of many you will encounter in this book: The metric/US needle size chart. The US has its own system while the rest of the world uses metric.

Metric (in mm)	US	Metric (in mm)	US	Metric (in mm)	US
1.0	000	4.0	6	9.0	13
1.5	00	4.5	7	9.5	
2.0	0	5.0	8	10.0	15
2.25	1	5.5	9	12.75	17
2.5		6.0	10	16.0	19
2.75	2	6.5	10·5	19.0	35
3.0		7.0		20.0	36
3.25	3	7.5		25.0	50
3.5	4	8.0	11		
3.75	5	8.5			

Tools of the Trade: Yarn

There's a fabulous yarn in your LYS (local yarn store) in a fantastic color. You've finally found a pattern for the perfect sweater. Just a matter of grabbing the nearest needles and casting on, right? Nope. If only it were that easy. Just as with cooking, combining ingredients in the correct proportions is important for getting the mix right.

Yarn is the umbrella term we use for all types of knitting fibers. Sheep's wool is the most well-known fiber spun into yarn, but it's really just a small part of what's available today. We get a lot of yarn from other animals as well, including goats, rabbits, alpacas, camels and silkworms. Cotton, linen and hemp are all-natural plant cellulose, while viscose takes natural materials and adds chemical elements. Technology has also given us completely artificial yarn that is a byproduct of petroleum: polyester. Add combinations or blends of fibers and you end up with an almost endless range of yarns.

How do you choose?

Knitting patterns always recommend a type of yarn or even a specific brand. This recommendation is in no way random, as the designers take the properties of the yarn into consideration when designing a garment. For instance, you probably won't see a cashmere summer T-shirt, because cashmere is wonderfully warm. When you're knitting from a pattern, the *safest* bet is to use the exact yarn listed. But as Knitchicks, we rarely go the safest route! If you plan to substitute a different yarn, you should choose one with similar properties. To give you a clear understanding of fiber properties, we've laid out an overview for you.

Animal Fibers

Alpaca: Indigenous to South America, the alpaca is part of the camel family (it's often confused with a llama). Lightweight and silky, like human hair, alpaca has no fluff.

Angora: The Angora rabbit produces the fiber used to make this yarn, which has a fluffy halo. Angora fiber is very soft, and yarns made from it can shed.

Cashmere: This fine, light, soft and warm fiber is taken from the undercoat (not guard hair) of the cashmere goat, a breed that originated in the Himalayas. It's quite expensive!

Mohair: Strong, elastic, shiny and fluffy, this woollike fiber comes from the Angora goat.

Merino: Merino fiber is wool fiber that comes from the merino breed of sheep. It's the finest and softest variety of wool.

Silk: This shiny, soft fiber actually comes from a protein filament spun by the silkworm to form its cocoon.

Plant Fibers

Cotton: Cotton yarn is spun from plant cellulose. It can be hard on the fingers, but it produces a breathable fabric.

Linen: This durable and lightweight fiber comes from the flax plant.

Bamboo: A relatively new player on the fiber scene, bamboo fiber is made from cellulose in the bamboo stalk. Bamboo fiber has properties similar to linen and cotton, plus it has nifty antibacterial properties.

Synthetic Fibers

Polyester: This artificial fiber is very strong and easy to wash—you can throw it in the washing machine.

Rayon: This soft yarn drapes well, but it has no stretch at all! Rayon comes from processed wood pulp called viscose. Bamboo fiber is also processed with a chemical in a similar fashion.

Blends

Blends are a great way to get the best of all worlds! For example, a 50% wool and 50% polyester blend creates a woolly yet strong yarn that can be thrown in the washing machine. Mixing cashmere with other fibers creates soft yarn that's more affordable and easier to maintain. Combining a fluffy fiber such as angora with another fiber ensures it sheds less. The combinations are endless.

Types of yarn

The choice of yarn does not end with the fiber. The way this fiber is spun or produced (processed) is also important.

Ply: A ply is a single strand of yarn. Most yarns are made of multiple, twined plies. For example, a two-ply yarn is made up of two strands.

Spiral/twist: To make fiber into yarn, it must be spun. When the fiber is created by twisting it to the left, it's called an S twist. When twisted to the right, it's a Z twist.

Bouclé: This yarn has a knobbly look created by one of its multiple strands being longer than the others.

Chenille: This fuzzy yarn has a thick woven core with short fibers around it.

Tape/ribbon: Just as the name suggests, this is flat yarn.

Cabled: Multiple-ply yarn that is plied together is called cabled yarn.

Slub: Irregular in shape, slub yarn is thick and thin in different spots.

It's Not Heavy, It's Yarn

Despite the name, "yarn weight" doesn't mean how much a ball weighs. Rather it refers to the thickness of the yarn. Yarns range from strands so fine it looks like you could floss your teeth with it to so chunky you could almost wrap it around your neck as a scarf without even bothering to knit it.

There are many systems of labeling yarn weight that seem to differ according to where you live. The Antipodeans use a ply method, the United Kingdom and United States have individual systems that sometimes use crossover words with differing meanings, and there's no system at all on the continent. The Craft Yarn Council of America has instituted a nomenclature to even things up *(Vogue Knitting* uses this in its patterns), but it has not been universally adopted.

The Craft Yarn Council of America issues many helpful charts on their Web site (www.craftyarncouncil.com) and the Standard Weight System shown below is no exception. Gauge is given over 4" (10cm) of Stockinette stitch.

	SUPER BULKY (6)	BULKY (5)	MEDIUM (4)	LIGHT (3)	FINE (2)	SUPERFINE (1)	LACE (0)
TYPE	bulky, roving	chunky, craft, rug	worsted, afghan, aran	dk, light, worsted	sport, baby	sock, fingering, baby	fingering, 10-count crochet thread
KNIT GAUGE RANGE	6–11 sts	12–15 sts	16–20 sts	21–24 sts	23–26 sts	27–32 sts	33–40 sts
RECOMMENDED NEEDLE IN US SIZE RANGE	11 and larger	9 to 11	7 to 9	5 to 7	3 to 5	1 to 3	000 to 1

Considering Gauge

So what does all this mean when you're choosing yarn for your project? It means you'll have to carefully choose a yarn-and-needle combination that produces the gauge recommended in the pattern. If you don't match up your gauge to the recommended gauge in the pattern, you'll have to recalculate to get the correct numbers of stitches and rows. Depending on the tension of your knitting, the gauge can change. Which is why—that's right, here comes the broken record—it's important to check your gauge by knitting a swatch with your yarn and needles of choice per project.

The Yarn Label

There's a wealth of information on the yarn label, and it's there for a reason: to guide you. Take note of the following information given on the yarn label and compare it to your pattern:

- manufacturer
- name of yarn
- fiber content
- actual weight
- length (yardage)
- recommended needle and gauge
- shade
- dye lot
- care instructions

Here's a tip: When purchasing multiple skeins of yarn, make sure all the yarn comes from the same dye lot—there can be subtle differences in color that might not be obvious to the naked eye but will definitely show up mid-sweater.

But There's No Label

What if you've lost the label, bought it from a local producer or just can't read the language? Use the Wraps Per Inch (WPI) method of determining weight (most commonly used by spinners). To do this, wrap the yarn around a WPI tool, a pencil or similar, ensuring that the yarn is evenly spaced with each strand touching the next (not too loose and not too tight). Now measure this against a ruler or check it against a handy wraps-per-inch chart (see below).

Ply	Yarn Weight	St/inch	WPI
2-ply	lace, laceweight	33–40	18+
3-ply	superfine, fingering, sock	27–32	16
4-ply	fine, baby, sport	23–26	14
8-ply	light, dK, sport/light worsted	21–24	12
10-ply	medium, aran, worsted	16–20	11
12-ply	heavy worsted	17–18	11
14-ply	chunky, bulky	12–15	10
15+-ply	bulky, superbulky	6–11	8

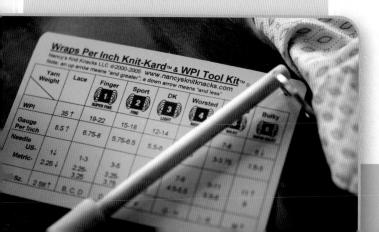

Applying a Gentle Touch: Caring for Yarn

Before you take that yarn home with you, make sure to check one more thing on the label: the care instructions. If you're knitting a kid's sweater, do you really want to make it in a fiber that's handwash only? Here's a quick guide to reading the cryptic symbols.

Washing

 Washing
Handwash in lukewarm water.

 Handwash in warm water.

 Don't handwash or machine wash.
(How do I keep it clean, then?)

 You can use chlorine/bleach.

 Don't bleach!

 This symbol indicates the machine cycle; it may also indicate the optimal temperature for the water.

 Don't dry clean.

 Go ahead and dry clean.

 Only dry clean with fluorocarbon or petroleum-based solutions.

 Only dry clean with perchlorethylene, fluorocarbon or petroleum-based solutions.

Drying

 Lay flat.

 You can dry in the dryer.

 Don't use the machine.
Let air-dry.

Ironing

 One dot means use a cool iron.

 Two dots mean use a warm iron.

 Three dots mean make it hot.

 Don't iron! Yay!

Tools of the Trade: Notions

Notions may seem indispensable, but Marcelle doesn't remember her mom having many of the notions we think of as essential. Most of these notions are simply suggestions, not must-haves. Although, we *are* always big fans of having a cute bag to carry knitting.

Bobbins: When you're battling intarsia or fair isle projects, bobbins are the go-to to keep the yarn from tangling. The trick is to let them dangle behind the work. Wrapping yarn around a piece of cardboard or a barrette can work perfectly as a homemade bobbin.

Cable Hooks: These U-shaped or hook-shaped needles are what we look to to hold stitches when we're working cables.

Crochet Hooks: Yes, we are knitters, but on occasion we'll go to our sister craft to help with threading fringes, fine tuning edges and hems, making picot embellishments and picking up dropped stitches.

Gauge Ruler: Pauline is a huge fan of these little knick knacks. Gauge rules are compact rulers that measure knit stitches over 4" (10cm). Many gauge rulers also contain holes for needle sizing.

Journals: We use journals to keep track of our schedules, so why not keep copious notes on our knitting habits? A well-kept knitting journal is a wonderful reference, short- and long-term!

Knitting Bag: The knitting bag we suggest is one that will carry your yarn and notions but not your copy of the latest tome by Susan Faludi. We suggest you choose a bag that's not too deep so things are easy to grab. Velcro is a destroyer of multi-ply yarn, so avoid it in your knitting bag. There are many stylish and functional knitting bags out on the market for you to choose from. Everyday handbags also work very well as knitting carry-alls, including backpacks.

Needle Cases: For those of us shy about using a vase as a needle holder, you can use needle cases to hold straight needles, circular needles, DPNs and crochet hooks. Sturdy, economical needle cases are out there, ready for the purchasing.

Point Protectors: You know how sometimes you reach into your bag to pull out your work and you pull the yarn off the needle instead? Point protectors stop this from happening; just stick them on the end of your needle. You can also use sponge bits that you cut yourself, a pencil eraser, or a simple rubber band. A point protector can be placed on one end of a DPN to turn it into a short straight needle.

Pom-Pom Makers: These can be a goddess-send for those of us completely unable to create pom-poms. They're easy to work with, instead of all the fumbling you may endure otherwise; of course, you can make one of these yourself out of cardboard.

Pouches/Minis: Small, zippered bags are wonderful for holding small accessories. Marcelle recycles make-up bags to carry around little notions, and zip-top freezer bags to corral buttons and such.

Row Counters: Marcelle is the first to admit that she loses count of rows when she's watching her favorite show. Row counters are a dream come true, as you are forced to pay attention to where you are at all times. This short-attention span issue Marcelle has is why she swears by knitting journals as well. Row counters are as compact as most notions go, which is all you can ask for when you start piling up the notions quotient!

Scissors: There's snipping to be done when you are a knitter. Getting a small pair of handy-dandy scissors is what we strongly urge you to do. For those of you who travel, there are also notched yarn cutters; they look like flat buttons and are as sharp as a hair dresser's shears.

Stitch Holders: Many knitters will use scrap yarn to function as a stitch holder, but you can also use the ones you find at your Local Yarn Store. They will take good care of your live stitches!

Stitch Markers: These round rings slip in between your stitches on the needle. The thinner your stitch marker, the better. It's best to use the ones that clip on and off. Small pieces of yarn can be used as stitch markers, and safety pins work well as they are quite thin. Think of stitch markers as your project's jewelry.

Tape Measure: Well, we all know how important measuring is to your project, don't we? Even our grandmums carried a tape measure around. This notion is one of the few musts on your list of notions.

Tapestry Needles: They sound fancy, but they're basically sewing needles with eyes large enough to accommodate the bulkiest of yarns. They're excellent seaming devices and are not at all sharp.

Knitchicks' Basics: Techniques

Let's get back to the basics for a minute with our take on beginnings, middles and ends. We'll cover everything from the very beginning—making a slip knot and a few cast-on methods—to the bitter end, including casting off and weaving in ends. We'll also show you how to knit and purl both the Continental and English ways so you can choose what's most comfortable for you.

IN THE BEGINNING...THE FIRST STITCH

The first stitch for a knitting project is always a slip knot. You create a slip knot with your fingers—there's no need to pick up your needles just yet! With practice, you'll be able to do this with your eyes closed.

MAKING A SLIP KNOT

FIGURE 1

FIGURE 2

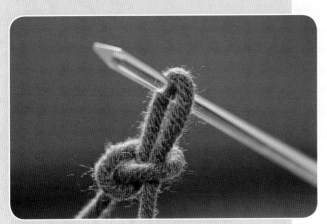

FIGURE 3

FIGURE 4

1. MAKE LOOP

Pull 10" (25cm) of yarn from the ball, leaving the yarn attached to the skein. Fold the yarn in half and twist it so the tail end is in front of the end still attached to the ball, creating a loop (Figure 1).

2. DRAW WORKING YARN THROUGH LOOP

The yarn attached to the ball is called the working yarn. The end of the yarn is the tail. Using your hands (no needle yet!), draw the working yarn through the loop (Figure 2). Voilà—you have a loop.

3. SLIDE LOOP ONTO NEEDLE

Slide the loop onto the needle, keeping it nice and loose (Figure 3). Then snug up the loop a bit so we can get on to the cast on (Figure 4)!

Helpful Hint About Tails

We recommend leaving a tail that is approximately 5" (13cm) long. A long tail comes in handy when and if you need to do some additional seaming when you're finishing your project. If you use the tail for seaming, you won't have to weave it in!

CASTING ON

Casting on creates the first row of stitches on your needle. There are a variety of ways to cast on; choose the method you'd like to use according to the piece you are making and your comfort level.

Different cast ons do create different effects. Some cast-on techniques create a stretchy edge, some are neater than others and some are just easy. If a pattern calls for a certain cast on, there's probably a reason for it, but if you're not comfortable with that method, do some test runs. There is no rule that says you must cast on as instructed. Remember, you are knitting to your comfort level.

WHAT IS ALL THE FUSS ABOUT ENGLISH AND CONTINENTAL?

There's a lot of noise about whether you knit holding your yarn with the right hand (English method) or whether you hold the yarn with your left hand (Continental method). Seriously. We'd like to do away with this altogether and call it what it really is about: Picking (the Continental method, which is really about the way you insert one needle into the other—you pick at the stitch) and throwing (the English method, which is more about the way you wrap the yarn around the needle before you begin each stitch: It's a dramatic throw, which the pickers don't do, as they're more Zen).

CASTING ON MULTIPLE STITCHES

While casting on usually happens at the beginning of a piece, there may be times when you need to increase stitches in the middle of a project. The following information will come in handy later when you begin working the projects in this book.

You can cast on at the beginning, end or even in the middle of a row. Increasing at the beginning of a row is simply achieved by casting on the required number of stitches using the knit on (see page 22), cable cast on (see page 23) or backward-loop method (see page 19). Increasing at the end of a row rarely happens because all you have to do is turn the piece around and the end becomes a new beginning!

You may need to increase (or make) more than one stitch in the middle of a row if you are shaping for an underarm or buttonhole. This will usually mean that you have cast off on a previous row, which requires you to cast on the same number of stitches as were cast off. Use the backward-loop (see page 19), knit on (see page 22) or cable cast-on method (see page 23), unless another cast on is specified in the pattern.

BACKWARD-LOOP (SIMPLE) METHOD

The backward-loop method is also known as single or simple cast on, and it is merely a line of loops on your needle.

— Good for items that need to have a lot of give (for example, top-down socks) or for casting on additional stitches in the middle of a row; can also be used for a temporary, or provisional, cast on

— Bad for when you want a nice, neat edge

— Pro: You only need one needle for this method, and when you get into a rhythm, it's really fast (especially when you're casting on a high number of stitches)

— Con: The first row is more difficult to knit—it's easy to drop stitches—so it may not be the best for beginners

1. MAKE LOOP

Make a slip knot (Figure 1). Circle the working yarn counterclockwise to make a loop around the needle with the yarn (Figure 2).

2. TIGHTEN LOOP ON NEEDLE

Slide the loop onto the needle and pull it tight (Figure 3). If you've looped the yarn the wrong direction, the yarn will slip off when you pull tight. Continue looping the yarn around the needle until you've cast on the required number of stitches.

FIGURE 1

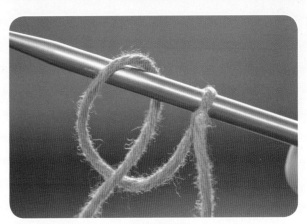

FIGURE 2

Helpful Hint About Tension

When casting on, don't pull too hard on the yarn as you will be creating a very, very tight row, which will result in too-tight stitches. If you are by nature a knitter with tight tension, use a needle two sizes larger than recommended for the cast on; you can go back to the recommended needle size once you've cast on.

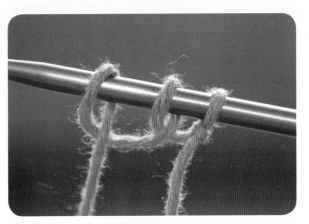

FIGURE 3

LONG-TAIL METHOD

The long-tail method uses the long tail of your slip knot to create the cast-on row. Make sure to calculate the appropriate length of the tail—if you guesstimate you may have to start over.

— Good for garments with Stockinette stitch or ribbed edges

— Bad for purl stitch starts

— Pro: Easy peasy and quick to do, and easy to start knitting from

— Con: If you underestimate the necessary length of the long tail, you have to start all over again

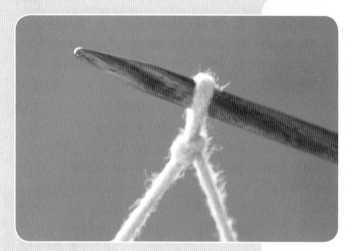

FIGURE 1

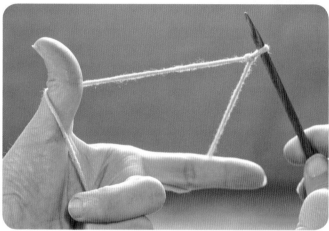

FIGURE 2

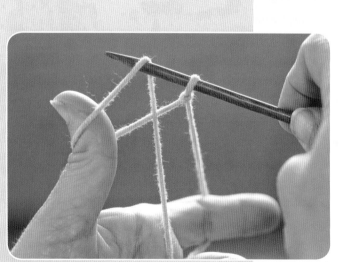

FIGURE 3

1. MAKE A SLIP KNOT WITH A LONG TAIL

Make a slip knot, leaving a long tail (Figure 1). The rule of thumb is to leave a tail approximately 3 times the width of the finished product. For instance, if the piece will be 4" (10cm) wide, leave a 12" (30cm) long tail. Don't forget to leave extra tail for weaving in.

2. POSITION YARN IN LEFT HAND

Hold the needle with the slip knot in your right hand, and grasp the yarn in your left hand, making a "thumbs up" sign. The working yarn should be in front, wrapped around your thumb. The tail is in the back, wrapped around your index finger. Secure both strands with your remaining fingers to create tension (Figure 2).

3. GRAB YARN WITH NEEDLE

Bring the needle in front of the yarn on your thumb and grab the yarn with the needle (Figure 3).

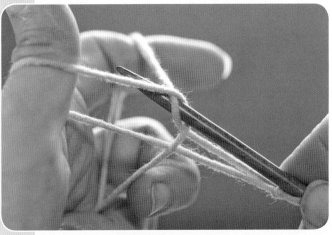

FIGURE 4

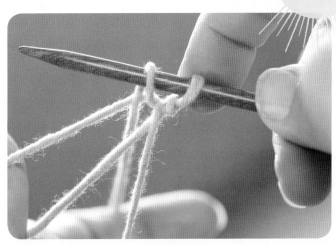

FIGURE 5

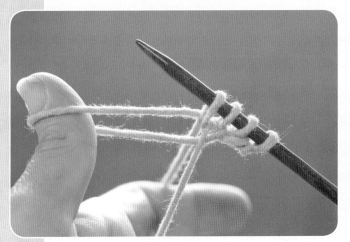

FIGURE 6

FIGURE 7

4. PULL LOOP ONTO NEEDLE

Bring the needle behind the yarn on your index finger and grab it with the needle. Pull the yarn back through the loop created by your thumb and the needle (Figure 4).

5. TIGHTEN LOOP ON NEEDLE

Once the loop (first stitch) is on the needle, allow the loop around your thumb to drop off and pull the 2 strands of yarn so the loop is snug around the needle (Figure 5).

6. CREATE STITCH

Repeat Steps 2–5 to create as many stitches as required for the cast-on row (Figures 6 and 7).

KNIT ON

Knitting on is the most straightforward cast-on method: It's the same technique as knitting and requires both needles.

— Good for any visible edges

— Bad for anything that needs to have considerable give, or anything that must be loose

— Pro: Know this cast on, and you've got the knit stitch down

— Con: It's a bit more complicated than the backward-loop and long-tail methods

FIGURE 1

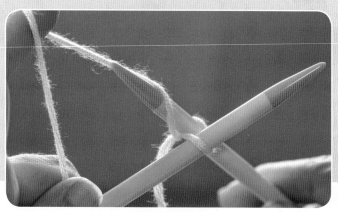

FIGURE 2

FIGURE 3

1. INSERT NEEDLE THROUGH STITCH FROM FRONT TO BACK

Make a slip knot and slide it on the needle. Hold the needle with the slip knot in your left hand. Insert the tip of the right needle into the front of the loop, from right to left and front to back (Figure 1).

2. WRAP YARN AROUND NEEDLE

Wrap the yarn counterclockwise around the right needle (Figure 2). Although the Continental method is shown here, this cast on can also be done using the English method.

3. PULL YARN THROUGH TO CREATE NEW STITCH

Bring the right needle through the loop on the left needle, grabbing the wrapped yarn and pulling it through (Figure 3). Note that at this point on a knit stitch (when you're knitting, not casting on), you'd push the loop off the left needle. Do not do this! Bring the right needle toward you (approximately 1½" [4cm]) and then to the right. You have created an elongated loop on the right needle.

4. INSERT NEEDLE INTO LOOP

Slip the left needle into this stitch from left to right. Remove the right needle and pull the yarn (not too tight) (Figure 4). Note that some knitters prefer to transfer the loop across without the twist.

FIGURE 4

CABLE CAST ON

The cable cast on is Pauline's favorite way to cast on. It gives the neatest finish of all and still has a fair bit of spring. It starts off the same way as the knit on cast on, but you insert the needle between two stitches instead of into the last stitch.

— Good for ribbing at the bottom of a garment and for creating a very smooth cast-on edge

— Bad for socks

— Pro: The cast-on edge has a well-defined line

— Con: It's a bit challenging at first, because knitting between stitches seems counterintuitive

FIGURE 1

FIGURE 2

1. KNIT ON 2 STITCHES AND INSERT NEEDLE TIP BETWEEN STITCHES

To begin, cast on 2 stitches onto your needle with the knit on method (see page 22). Next, instead of putting the needle tip into the front of the next stitch, insert it between the 2 cast-on stitches (Figures 1 and 2).

2. WRAP YARN AROUND NEEDLE

Follow the same steps as for knitting on to create stitches, wrapping the yarn around the needle (Figure 3), pulling it through the loop (Figure 4) and twisting and moving the loop to the left needle. This cast on can be done using either the Continental or English method.

FIGURE 3

FIGURE 4

THE MIDDLE...KNITTING AND PURLING

When it comes down to the basics of knitting, it's all about the knit stitch and the purl stitch. Everything flows from these two stitches. Even the fanciest of stitches are simply variations of the knit stitch and the purl stitch. So once you've got knit and purl sorted, you're sorted!

THE KNIT STITCH

The knit stitch is the foundation of all knitting. It's a V-shaped stitch, and the "lid" of the V links behind the one above it, creating a smooth finish.

Knitting the English Way: Throwing

OK, so we're not exactly throwing, nor even English. The "throw" bit comes from the working yarn being wrapped (or thrown) around the needle. The "English" part is to distinguish it from what was done on the Continent (mainland Europe).

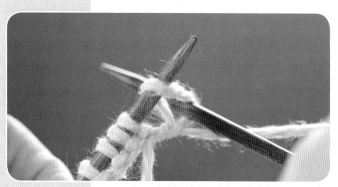

FIGURE 1

FIGURE 2

FIGURE 3

1. INSERT RIGHT NEEDLE INTO FIRST STITCH

Hold the needle with the cast-on stitches in your left hand and the empty needle in your right. The working yarn (attached to the ball) comes from behind your knitting. Insert the tip of the right needle into the first stitch on the left needle, from right to left and front to back (Figure 1).

2. WRAP YARN AROUND RIGHT-HAND NEEDLE

Holding the yarn in your right hand, wrap it counterclockwise around the right-hand needle (Figure 2).

3. PULL YARN THROUGH STITCH

Bring the right-hand needle through the loop on the left needle, pulling the wrapped yarn through the stitch (Figure 3). This step is the hard one: It helps to picture the needles perpendicular to each other toward the tip, the left on top of the right. Just slide the right-hand needle underneath the left-hand needle without losing contact. Slide the right-hand needle to the right, away from the left-hand needle, pushing the original stitch off (it's now sitting underneath the new stitch created).

Helpful Hint

Pauline's got a jingle she teaches to her students; it comes in handy when you forget how to do the knit stitch: "In through the front door and around the back, out through the window and off jumped Jack."

Knitting the Continental Way: Picking

When you've learned to knit one way, you may not even know there's another way until you see other knitters working differently than you do. That was the case for Marcelle. If you push your needle into the stitch to wrap it, you're a picker, also known as a knitter who knits the Continental way.

FIGURE 1

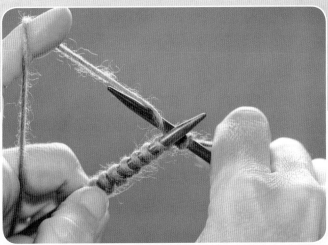

FIGURE 2

FIGURE 3

FIGURE 4

1. INSERT RIGHT NEEDLE INTO FIRST STITCH

Hold the needle with the cast-on stitches in your left hand, and at the same time, drape the working yarn (attached to the ball) over your left index finger. Create tension on the yarn by holding it with the remaining fingers of your left hand. Hold the empty needle in your right hand. Insert the tip of the right-hand needle into the first stitch on the left-hand needle, from right to left and front to back (Figure 1).

2. SCOOP YARN

"Scoop" the yarn on your index finger by dipping the needle to wrap the yarn around the needle counterclockwise (Figure 2). Bring the yarn back through the loop and bring it forward (in front of the left needle). This "scooped" yarn now forms a loop sitting on your right needle (Figure 3).

3. DROP OLD STITCH OFF NEEDLE

Slide the right needle to the right, away from the left, pushing the original stitch off (it's now sitting underneath the new stitch created) (Figure 4).

THE PURL STITCH

The purl stitch is the knit stitch, but from behind! In its V shape, the "lid" of the V links in front of the one above it, creating a bumpy finish. When you're knitting traditional Stockinette, the purl side is often referred to as the Wrong Side (WS) and has the bar formation instead of the V.

Purling the English Way: Throwing

It's just like knitting the English Way, except, well, you're purling. Go figure! And Marcelle has to confess, she can't knit a stitch of the English (throwing) method.

FIGURE 1

FIGURE 2

FIGURE 3

FIGURE 4

1. INSERT RIGHT NEEDLE INTO FIRST STITCH

Insert the tip of the right-hand needle into the front of the first stitch on the left-hand needle, from right to left and back to front (Figure 1).

2. WRAP YARN AROUND NEEDLE

Use your right hand to wrap the yarn counterclockwise around the right needle (Figure 2).

3. PULL YARN THROUGH STITCH

Slip the right-hand needle through the loop on the left-hand needle, bringing the wrapped yarn through (Figures 3 and 4). Slide the right-hand needle underneath the left-hand needle from front to back without losing contact. Slide the right-hand needle to the right, away from the left-hand needle, pushing the original stitch off (it's now sitting underneath the new stitch created).

Purling the Continental Way: Picking

Purling continental (picking the stitches) is a very subtle operation. It's dipping in to catch the stitch, without the dramatic flair of wrapping yarn.

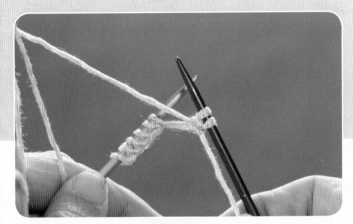

FIGURE 1

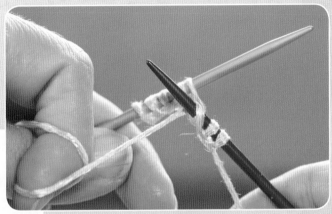

FIGURE 2

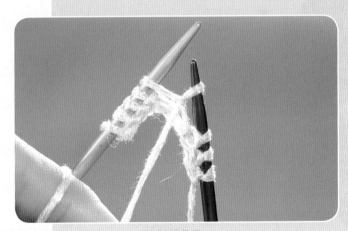

FIGURE 3

1. INSERT RIGHT NEEDLE INTO FIRST STITCH

Hold the needle with the cast-on stitches in your left hand, and at the same time, drape the working yarn (attached to the ball) over your left index finger, coming in front of your knitting (Figure 1). Hold the empty needle in your right hand. Insert the tip of the right needle into the front of the first stitch on the left needle from right to left and back to front.

2. WRAP YARN AROUND NEEDLE

Wrap the yarn on your left index finger counterclockwise around the right-hand needle (Figure 2).

3. PULL YARN THROUGH STITCH

Slide the tip of the right-hand needle back out of the loop, bringing the wrapped yarn with it to create a new stitch (Figure 3). Slide the right-hand needle away from the left-hand needle, dropping the old stitch off the needle and leaving the new stitch on the right needle.

Minding Your Knits and Purls

When you knit a row, then purl a row, and then repeat, you are knitting in Stockinette stitch.

When you knit every row, you are knitting in garter stitch.

THE SHAPE OF THINGS TO COME... INCREASING AND DECREASING

As knitters, we take up knitting scarves because they are simple: a lot of knitting back and forth and not much more. For many knitters, shaping is intimidating. Oh sure, we'll take on hats—after all, they're small and require less sweat. The thing about sweaters is this: they challenge you! They test your math skills, your knitting knowledge and your shaping savvy. Sounds hard, right? Well, there's another way to look at this. Shaping is about two things: increasing and decreasing the number of stitches you're working. And because knitting and purling are the foundation of all other knitting techniques, increasing and decreasing are nothing more than variations of a skill you already know. The point is: You can do it.

INCREASING

As with most things in knitting, there are many different ways to increase. You can increase using method A or method B, and you'll always produce the same result: an extra stitch. The key is to learn these methods so you can decide which to use for the task at hand.

Yarn Over

The easiest type of increase is a yo (yarn over), also called a yf (yarn forward). Yarn overs are most commonly used to create lacy patterns. So, if you're trying to add stitches in a subtle manner, this is not the technique you'll want to use.

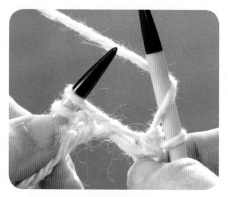

FIGURE 1

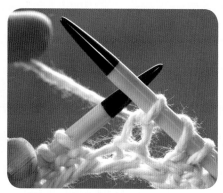

FIGURE 2

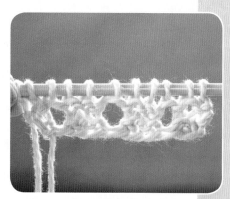

FIGURE 3

1. BRING YARN OVER NEEDLE

On a knit stitch, a yarn over is created by wrapping the yarn around the needle by bringing the yarn to the front, then over the needle (Figure 1). The next stitch is knit as normal, leaving a loop (Figure 2). On a purl stitch, the yarn is already at the front. Wrap it counterclockwise around the needle and purl as normal, again leaving a loop between the stitches.

2. WORK SERIES OF YARN OVERS

Note that a YO looks different from the other stitches as it appears slanted and not anchored to a stitch below. Keep this in mind when you come to work this stitch on the next row: It can easily slip off. The other thing to keep in mind about the YO/YF is that it creates a small hole in the knitted piece. This can be used to a pleasant decorative effect (Figure 3).

Knit or Purl in Front or Back

Another common increase is the KFB or PFB (knit or purl in front and back), also called a bar increase. In this stitch, you use both the "front" and "back" leg of the stitch.

1. KNIT INTO FRONT OF STITCH

On the knit side, first knit the stitch, but don't slip it off of the left-hand needle (Figure 1).

2. KNIT INTO BACK OF STITCH

Bring the right-hand needle back behind the left one and knit into the back part of the stitch (Figure 2). Finish the stitch and slip it off the left needle. You've created 2 new stitches instead of just 1. On the purl side, you'll work a PFB (purl front and back). Purl the front loop as normal, but do not slip it off the needle. Return the right needle to the back and purl from behind the back loop (bringing the needle from the left to the right through the back of the stitch). You will have 1 normal-looking stitch, and the second stitch will have a horizontal line (or "bar") at its base.

FIGURE 1

FIGURE 2

Make One

A M1 (make one) is created by using the horizontal yarn between two stitches to create a new stitch. A standard Make 1 is created by knitting into the front of the picked up bar of yarn, which makes a hole that is smaller than a YO. There are also directional variations of Make 1 (M1L or M1R) that are created by twisting the picked-up bar of yarn; M1L and M1R do not leave a hole in the knitting.

1. PICK UP BAR WITH RIGHT-HAND NEEDLE

If you already have knitting on your needles, you will notice that there is a horizontal line between stitches. Pick up this bar with your right-hand needle by inserting the needle into the stitch front to back (Figure 1).

2. SLIP LOOP ONTO LEFT-HAND NEEDLE

For a standard Make 1, or a M1L, slip the loop of yarn onto your left-hand needle, keeping the yarn oriented from front to back (Figure 2). For a M1R, slip the loop of yarn onto your left-hand needle with the left part of the loop forward.

3. KNIT INTO LOOP

For a standard Make 1, knit through the front of the loop of yarn as you would any knit stitch. For a M1L, knit the new stitch through the back instead of dipping down and picking into it (Figure 3). For M1R, knit through the front of the stitch, which will be twisted on the needle.

FIGURE 1

FIGURE 2

FIGURE 3

Helpful Hint

If you have trouble remembering whether it is the front or the back you should be knitting into for M1L, choose the more difficult option and you'll be right every time!

DECREASING

We love decreasing—it's less fussy than increasing. What you do need to keep in mind is whether your decrease will slope to the left or right. So bookmark this page, and refer to it if you forget: knit two together (k2tog) creates a right-sloping decrease and decreases that involve slipping a stitch create a left-sloping one.

Knit or Purl Two Together

When you see k2tog or p2tog, you know what's coming: the right-sloping decrease.

FIGURE 1

K2TOG (KNIT 2 TOGETHER)

To k2tog, slide your right needle into the front loops of the next 2 stitches, just as you would for a regular knit stitch (Figure 1). Knit the 2 stitches as usual, holding them together. This action decreases 1 stitch.

P2TOG (PURL 2 TOGETHER)

P2tog is similarly made by scooping up 2 stitches with your right needle and purling them as if they were one, resulting in a right-slanting decrease of 1 stitch.

Slip, Slip, Knit (SSK)

This decrease slopes to the left, as does the sl 1, k1, psso (slip one, knit one, pass slipped stitch over), which you'll tackle in some of the patterns. The slip is exactly how it sounds: Simply slide the stitch from one needle to the other as if to knit—that's it.

FIGURE 1

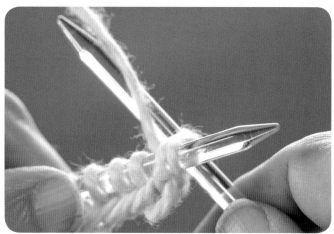

FIGURE 2

SSK (SLIP ONE, SLIP ONE, KNIT TWO TOGETHER)

Slip the first stitch onto the right-hand needle, slip the second stitch onto the right-hand needle (both as if to knit) (Figure 1). Then insert the left needle into the fronts of these 2 stitches from left to right and knit them together (Figure 2).

THE END...BINDING OFF AND SEAMING UP

This is the part of the project where you think you are done, but no, you are not. Binding off is the beginning of the finishing. After you bind off, you'll need to seam everything up. And then there's the weaving—the cleanup aspect of finishing.

BINDING OFF (CASTING OFF)

Binding off is the process of ending a piece of knitting by securing the stitches so they don't unravel. There aren't as many choices for binding off as for casting on; the simple style shown here works well in most situations.

FIGURE 1

FIGURE 2

FIGURE 3

1. PASS FIRST STITCH OVER SECOND

Knit 2 stitches very loosely (Figure 1). With your left needle, insert the tip into the front loop of the first stitch you knitted on the right needle (Figure 2). Pick up this stitch, carry it over the second stitch and let it drop off both needles (Figure 3). You have bound off 1 stitch, and there is still 1 stitch on your right needle.

2. PASS FIRST STITCH OVER SECOND AGAIN

Knit another stitch so there are again 2 stitches on your right-hand needle. Repeat the process of picking up the first stitch on the right needle (the one farthest from the tip of the needle), carrying it over

the other stitch and dropping it off of both needles. Continue in this way until you have 1 stitch remaining on your right needle, and none on your left.

3. SECURE FINAL STITCH

Cut the yarn at least 5" (13cm) away from the last stitch. Pull the loop a bit to enlarge it and remove the needle. Thread the yarn tail through this loop and pull it to secure. The tail that is left will be woven in at the end. If this bound-off edge is a seam, make the tail longer so it can be used to sew the pieces together.

Helpful Hint

You will not necessarily always bind off on a knit row. If you are casting off on a purl row, the process is the same using a purl stitch: Purl 2, pick up the first purled stitch and carry it over the second purled stitch, and drop it off the needle. Continue as instructed in Binding Off. Likewise with ribbing: Knit the knit stitches and purl the purl stitches, dropping the first stitch over and off the second one. Continue as instructed in Binding Off.

Helpful Hint: Binding Off Mid-Row

When working the front of a sweater, you will often bind off in the middle of a row as you shape the neck. This can be a minefield of errors if you don't keep your notes copiously detailed. So do that. Also, don't hesitate to work one side first, then the other side. Very often in patterns, you'll see the confusing "work both sides at once" instruction. We recommend working one side, seeing how that turns out and then proceeding to the other side.

SEWING UP: YOUR INNER SEAMSTRESS

As with so much in knitting, there are a variety of ways to sew up your bits. And when we say bits, we're talking sewing sleeves to the body of the project or sewing the collar onto it. On this page, we show you the two most common seaming techniques: mattress stitch and Kitchener stitch. All you need is a yarn needle (sometimes called a tapestry needle) to seam knitted pieces together.

Mattress Stitch

Mattress stitch is always worked on the right side of the knitting. It creates an invisible seam.

SEAMING PIECES FACING THE SAME DIRECTION

When seaming the sides of a sweater together, first line up the 2 pieces stitch-for-stitch. Starting 1 stitch in from the edge, insert the needle and pick up 2 bars (it doesn't matter if it's in the middle of a stitch, or between stitches) and pull the yarn through. Move the needle over to the other side and do the same (Figure 1).

SEAMING PIECES FACING DIFFERENT DIRECTIONS

When joining the sleeves to the body, 1 piece will be facing up, and the other will be facing sideways. To seam 2 pieces facing in different directions, start with the horizontal piece, and pick up 2 bars of the stitch across from it. Now bring the needle to the vertical piece and pick up the V of the stitch (Figure 2).

FIGURE 1   **FIGURE 2**

Kitchener Stitch

The beauty of the Kitchener stitch is that it leaves no seam at all. The difficulty is that there is a rhythm you need to follow. This can be a tricky technique to learn, so we've used illustrations to make everything crystal clear. Take this technique one step at a time and you'll be just fine.

You may hear fellow knitters refer to Kitchener as grafting, which is an accurate description of what Kitchener is: joining live stitches with a tapestry needle. Before Kitchener can begin, you must prep. Be certain you have the same number of stitches on each needle. There's no room for leftover stitches with Kitchener. If the number of stitches is not the same, you have some more knitting to do.

Hold the Wrong Sides of the work together with the Right Sides facing outward. If you have a long tail hanging off the work, use that, but check that the tail is in fact long enough—three times the length of the width of the work you are about to seam.

1. BRING NEEDLE THROUGH FIRST FRONT STITCH AS IF TO PURL

Insert the threaded tapestry needle into the first stitch on the needle closest to you as if to purl and pull it through, but leave the stitch on the needle (Figure 1).

2. BRING NEEDLE THROUGH FIRST BACK STITCH AS IF TO KNIT

Now insert the needle through the first stitch on the back needle as if to knit and pull the yarn through (Figure 2). Don't tighten tautly, and keep this in mind throughout the effort.

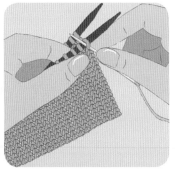
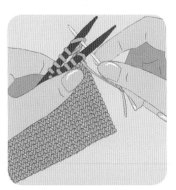

FIGURE 1   **FIGURE 2**

Begin Kitchener Stitch

The work is now ready to begin. You will be repeating steps 3 through 6 until the two pieces are fully connected.

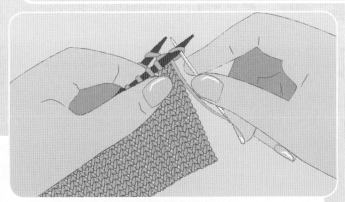

FIGURE 3

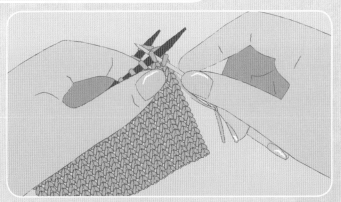

FIGURE 4

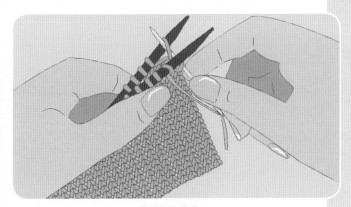

FIGURE 5

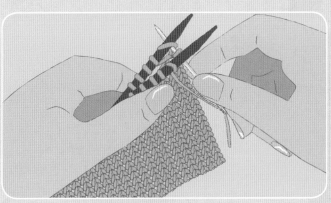

FIGURE 6

3. BRING NEEDLE THROUGH FIRST FRONT STITCH AS IF TO KNIT, SLIP OFF

Insert the needle into the first stitch on the front needle as if to knit, while slipping it off the end of the needle (Figure 3).

4. BRING NEEDLE THROUGH NEXT FRONT STITCH AS IF TO PURL

Insert the needle into the next stitch on the front needle as if to purl, but this time, leave it on the needle (Figure 4). Gently pull the yarn through.

5. INSERT NEEDLE THROUGH FIRST BACK STITCH AS IF TO PURL, SLIP OFF

Insert the needle into the first stitch on the back needle as if to purl, and slip it off the end of the needle (Figure 5).

6. BRING NEEDLE THROUGH NEXT BACK STITCH AS IF TO KNIT

Insert the needle into the next stitch on the back needle as if to knit, and leave it on the needle (Figure 6). Pull the yarn through. And that is Kitchener!

Helpful Hints for Kitchener Stitch

If Kitchener stitch was written as a pattern, it would read P1, k1, *k1, p1, p1, k1; repeat from * to end. Except you are threading here and not knitting!

Here are some other things to remember:

* The dropping off of a stitch occurs once it's been threaded through twice.

* Be certain to pull the threaded-through stitches off the needles before you embark on the next set.

* Keep your grafting yarn under the needles, not over.

* Singsong your way through this: knit purl front needle, purl knit back needle, pull it off!

* Concentrate!

You Say Jumper, I Say Sweater: Learning the Basics of Sweater Knitting

Pullover, sweater, jumper: whatever you call them, it's all about the top of your body. (And let's just clear something up: In the UK, Australia and a few other countries, a sweater is called a jumper.) What is universal is this: There are innumerable styles, methods and techniques for making a sweater—they can be knit from the top down, bottom up, sideways, flat or in the round. It's just a matter of what the pattern calls for or how you prefer to tackle a project.

Before you start the work of knitting a sweater, there is some prep involved, including choosing the pattern, the yarn and your finishing options. In this section, we give you a broad overview of this prep work. As you delve into the individual patterns, you'll pick up more and more techniques to add to your bag of skills.

CHOOSING YARN

Once you pick a pattern, the next step is to choose your yarn. Take into account the properties of the yarn (already discussed on pages 12–14) and also the quantity required for the project. Nothing is worse than running out of yarn in the middle of a project, especially if you discover your LYS has also run out! Don't forget to check dye lots when purchasing multiple skeins.

Swatch, Swatch, Swatch!

How to say this politely? Knit Test Swatches, Knitter! We know that you just want to get on with it and you've got this stash of yarn burning a hole in your knitting bag. But please believe us when we say that knitting a swatch will help you in the long run.

Knitting a test swatch is like a yarn test drive. It's your opportunity to determine gauge as well as to see how the yarn works with your stitch, your tension and your touch. Knitting a test swatch is even better if you put it to good use. Keeping good notes and attaching them to your swatch will be invaluable to you down the road. Our tried and true swatch-making tips make good use of your time: you get quite a bit of information from that small piece of knitting.

Size matters: Knit a 4" (10cm) square test swatch with the needles you plan to use for the project. Feel free to experiment and play with your needle sizes. Examine the fabric to decide which needles work best. If you are using a yarn other than the one the pattern recommends, compare your results to the pattern specifications to make sure you have a match.

Label your swatches: Write down all the vital swatch information on a piece of scrap paper or a sticky note, including the size of the needles you used, the row and stitch gauge over 4" (10cm) and the name of the yarn. Attach this paper to the swatch with a safety pin. You'll thank yourself later.

CHOOSING A FIT

With sweaters, there's a lot of talk about the fit. The way a sweater fits is really a matter of personal preference. Do you like your sweaters to fit you snugly, or do you want a little breathing room? When it comes to knitting sweaters, there are three general fits:

Close or Fitted Fit: The close fit is form-hugging. If you want to knit a fitted sweater, subtract between 2" (5cm) and 4" (10cm) from your actual measurements when calculating stitch counts.

Standard or Classic Fit: With a standard or classic fit, the sweater is not too snug and not too loose. To acheive a classic fit, add 2" (5cm) to your actual measurements when calculating stitch counts.

Loose or Oversized Fit: When a garment is loose or oversized, it's not so formfitting. If you're knitting a loose sweater, add 4" (10cm) to your actual measurements when calculating stitch counts.

Measuring Up and Down

When knitting a sweater, it's important to properly measure your bits before beginning a project. That way you'll know if you need to adjust the pattern to fit you correctly. There are several key measurements you should take:

1. Bust: Measure around the fullest part of your chest.

2. Waist: Measure around your waist at the narrowest point.

3. Hips: Measure around the fullest part of your hips.

4. Arms: Measure from the edge of the shoulder to the wrist. For three-quarter or short sleeves, measure from the edge of your shoulder to the point where you want the sleeve to fall.

5. Under (arms): Measure from the underarm to the wrist.

6. Upper arms: Measure around your upper arm.

7. Wrists: Measure around your wrist.

8. Neck: Measure around your neck.

9. Armhole: Measure from the top of the shoulder to the underarm.

10. Back: Measure from the top of the neck to the point where you want the bottom of the sweater to fall.

Helpful Hint

Use the measurements of one of your favorite jumpers (or, if you're making one for someone else, borrow one of their beloved sweaters) as a model for your knitting.

CHOOSING A NECKLINE

Many wearers of knitted sweaters are quite particular about their neckline preferences. Some of us prefer the plunge while others want to hide their chicken necks. As you delve into the patterns in this book, you'll encounter even more enticing ways to show off that clavicle.

Ballerina Neck: A sexy, classic scoop neck.

Boatneck: A wide neckline with a simple line that cuts across the neck. It's the same on the back and front.

Collar: A very stylized neckline. Many times, a pattern will have you knit a crew neck, then pick up stitches for the collar at the end.

Crew Collar: The standard round collar.

Turtleneck: Runs up your actual neck (and often folds back over again).

V-Neck: An often plunging neckline that's great for showing off that cleavage. Or not.

CHOOSING SLEEVES

Knitting sleeves is a double-edged sword. They require fewer stitches, so knitting them goes quickly. But you have to knit them twice. Even trickier, the second sleeve has to mirror the first exactly. We urge you to keep copious notes when knitting sleeves, jotting down the rows you've knit as you knit them, so as to keep track of the work you are doing. That way, when you knit the second sleeve you won't be wondering if you followed the pattern precisely or if you went "off script" a bit.

All the Raglan

The term raglan sweater refers to any sweater where the sleeves join the neckline and slant out from that point. As with just about all sweaters, it can be knit from the bottom up or from the top down. However, raglan sweaters are perfect for knitting in the round. Whichever way you choose, it all comes down to the Four Noble Tips.

1. You always work in thirds: The first two thirds are the front and back panels, and the final third is divided in half for the sleeves.

2. You are (generally) knitting in the round: Most raglan sweaters are knit in the round, although it is possible to knit a raglan-style cardigan by working back and forth. But why not knit a tube and cut a steek? (When you steek a sweater, you cut your knitting...don't worry, it's not as scary as it seems [see pages 106–107 to see how it's done].)

3. You'll increase (or decrease) quickly at the yoke: When working the top portion of the raglan, the secret is to increase (or decrease) two stitches at each stitch marker every other round.

4. You will need to do a fair bit of measuring and calculating: See the Choosing a Fit section, page 34, for specifics on the measurements needed.

Joining to Work in the Round on Circular Needles

The only trick to joining stitches to work in the round is to not twist your stitches! Before you join to work in the round, turn all the cast-on stitches to face the same direction—loops facing out and knotted side facing in. If you do accidentally twist the stitches, it will be a mistake you only make once! It cannot be fixed later and will need to be ripped out.

Helpful Hints: The Upkeep of Circular Needles

The tips of a circular needle are attached by a cord that can get a bit mangled after extensive use. Still, it's difficult to lay flat a 40" (102cm) circular needle to straighten it out. We prefer to lay them in needle cases. In lieu of a needle case, take a tip from the manufacturer for organizing circular needles: place them in labeled zippered plastic baggies.

If your plastic cord does get mangled, try dunking it in warm (not boiling!) water to loosen it up. Let the cord sit for two minutes and then stretch it out. Another method for straightening a kinked cord is to blow-dry it straight with a hair dryer set to low heat.

Joining to Work in the Round on Double-Pointed Needles

Once all the stitches are cast on and evenly distributed between the needles, check to make sure the stitches are not twisted. This can be hard to identify on DPNs, so lay them on a flat surface to check. After your stitches are straight, all you need to do is position the double-pointed needles so the last stitch and the first stitch (last and first needles) are next to one another and continue knitting, in much the same way as when you join stitches for working in the round on a circular needle.

Knitting in the Round with Double-Pointed Needles

Back in the day, knitting in the round was done exclusively with double-pointed needles. Today DPNs are most often associated with sock knitting, but did you know that people used to knit whole sweaters on them? Before the clever Norwegians invented circular needles at the beginning of the twentieth century, all knitting done in the round was on four or five long, double-pointed needles. A fourteenth century painting of the Madonna shows her doing just this! While DPNs may seem unwieldy or intimidating, they are great for knitting sleeves because most circular needles will not accommodate the small circumference.

With DPNs—just as with circulars—you knit in the round. DPNs come in sets of four or five, so that your knitting takes a triangular shape when distributed over three needles, with one working needle left over, or a square shape when distributed over four needles, with one working needle. Knit along the first needle, and you end up with a needle full of stitches in your right hand and an empty needle in your left. Then move on to the next needle (turning your knitting in a counterclockwise direction). The empty needle is now in your right hand, and you work through the next needle. Around and around you go, moving on to the next needle as each one empties.

Technically, knitting on DPNs requires no extra skill, just confidence! Of course it looks like you're wrestling with an octopus, but you're only ever using two needles at a time—the other needles just dangle until needed. Ignore them and concentrate on the ones right in front of you.

Things to Know about Using DPNs

- **Keep it straight:** You must be careful not to twist the stitches before joining for in-the-round knitting, just as with circulars.

- **Four versus five:** If you have lots of stitches, use five needles. Otherwise, use four or five needles depending on what feels best.

- **Distribute stitches evenly:** Place the same number of stitches on each needle (or as close as possible). If you are increasing or decreasing, transfer the stitches periodically to achieve equal distribution.

- **Keep good tension:** If your tension is correct, the stitches will not slide off the needles when you're not working them.

- **The first row is the toughest:** It can be a bit challenging to work the first row after the cast on. But after that, it's smoooooth sailing!

- **Easy transport:** You can fold up the needles by collapsing the circle and pushing the knitting to the center for hassle-free transport.

Things to Avoid when Using DPNs

- **The dreaded ladder:** A ladder, or awkward space between stitches, can sometimes form between two needles if the stitches don't sit together with the proper tension (when the piece is finished you can still tell where the needles were). To avoid ladders, on every needle simply pull the second stitch after the needle change tightly to even out the tension.

- **Wrong needle:** Pulling out the wrong needle is a common cause for shriek-

ing among knitters! It's easily done: You're knitting merrily along one needle, the left one empties of stitches, you go to transfer it...and grab the wrong one. All those just-knit stitches are hanging in the air! Double check before you transfer the working needle.

Transferring from Circulars to DPNS

As we know, increasing or decreasing stitches means our knitting will grow or shrink in width. Occasionally it will be necessary to change from circulars to DPNs (or vice versa) because the knitting no longer fits the needles. Although it can be cumbersome, it's not difficult.

Circulars to DPNs: If you're decreasing and your stitches no longer fit on your circular needles, don't stretch them out. Use DPNs instead. Divide the number of stitches by three or four, depending on how many DPNs you'll use. Then introduce one DPN at a time, with the circular needle in your left hand and the DPN in your right. When the first DPN is full, let it go. Pick up an empty DPN and repeat the process. Keep going until all the stitches are off your circular needle and onto the DPNs.

DPNs to circulars: If you've got so many stitches on your DPNs that they're beginning to mutiny, introduce a circular needle just as you would a new DPN. Knit across each needle, and, as it empties of stitches, lay it aside. When all the stitches are on the circular, put away the DPNs.

The Stair Step

If knitting in the round is like a spiral staircase, how do you know when you've left the first floor (row) and are on the second? It's something knitters call the "stair step" and it is most obvious on the cast on row or in stripes. Some people don't care about the stair step, and some do.

To eliminate the stair step, cast on one more stitch than the pattern calls for. When you come to the end of the first round, slip the extra stitch onto the left needle and knit it together with the first stitch.

To minimize the visibility of the stair step when knitting stripes, try bringing the stripe in at the shoulder stitch marker.

If seeing the mismatched stripes grates on you, you can employ the jogless join method. Join in the new color and knit and entire round. Just before you start the second round of the new color, pick up the stitch from the row below (the first stitch of the new color) and knit it together with the next one. Note that in doing this, you move the beginning of the round one stitch to the left each time a new color is introduced.

Converting Wrong Side to the Only Side You Know!

When working in the round, remember we're working rounds, not rows. This brings up the sticky subject of, Well-How-Do-I-Turn-A-Pattern-For-A-Flat-Piece-Into-One-For-The-Round?

A few key things to remember: To knit Stockinette stitch in the round, knit every single row. To knit garter, knit one row, purl the next and continue alternating. For repeating patterns, follow just the Right Side row instructions (if the background is Stockinette or reverse Stockinette). When knitting stitches such as a rib or seed stitch in the round, it's key to keep your eye on the rounds to ensure you are following the cadence of the stitch. For instance, when you're working in seed stitch, Round 1 will always be knit 1, purl 1 and Round 2 will always be purl 1, knit 1. If you can read the knitting, you don't even have to keep track—just knit the purls and purl the knits.

You may also need to add or subtract one or two stitches at the sides of sweaters where seams would usually be placed. To convert in-the-round patterns to flat, just follow the above advice in reverse.

Knitting Flat

Yes, the Knitchicks are sweet on knitting in the round, but we go flat, too.

When you knit flat, you work each piece separately, knitting back and forth and hopefully keeping track of the rows. Then comes the fun part: seaming it all up.

As you delve into the Knitchicks' patterns, you'll find all kinds of methods for seaming up your panels and sleeves. See pages 32–33, for step-by-step instructions on the two most common seaming techniques, mattress stitch and Kitchener stitch. Here are the basic steps you'll follow when knitting a sweater flat:

1. Select yarn
2. Calculate gauge
3. Get your gear in order (gather up all the notions and needles you will need for the project)
4. Take your measurements
5. Work the back panel
6. Work the front panel
7. Work the sleeves
8. Seam the pieces together (including seaming together front and back, and attaching sleeves)
9. Pick up stitches for hem, collar and cuffs
10. Finish it up (weave in ends)

Knitting Sleeves Flat

A sleeve knit "flat" is knit back and forth as a flat piece that will be seamed up later instead of as a seamless tube. Once the sleeve is knit, it's attached to the armhole, then the sleeve is seamed together. The best way to attach the sleeve to the armhole is to find the middle of the shoulder (if it's symmetrical, simply fold it in half to find the center) and the middle of the top of the armhole. Mark both center points and then pin the sleeve in place. Then do the same for the underarms. From there, you can sew the pieces together knowing they will fit together properly. Some garments require "ease," meaning the sleeve seems too big for the armhole. This discrepancy is deliberate to allow more room for your shoulders. As with all seaming, we recommend using the long tail from your cast on or bind off.

FINISHING UP

At the end of every pattern, you'll generally find a little heading that reads "Finishing." This is where you wrap things up by adding collars, hems and cuffs, by seaming together pieces, by closing up armholes and weaving in ends. Some people dread finishing, while others really enjoy it. Whether you love it or hate it, finishing is an essential part of the process.

Assembly Session

There are a couple of ways to sew up your seams, including mattress stitch and Kitchener stitch, otherwise known as grafting. When finishing a sweater, you should follow this general order of operations:

Knitting in the Round

1. Close up holes under arms
2. Weave in ends
3. Pick up stitches for collar and cuffs
4. Weave in ends

Knitting Flat

If you've knit your sweater flat, you'll first need to seam all the pieces together before picking up stitches for collar and cuff and weaving in ends. Seam the pieces together in this order:

1. Sew shoulder seams
2. Sew top of sleeve to shoulder
3. Fit armhole (make sure the armhole and the sleeve match up!)
4. Sew side seams, working from the hem up to the armhole
5. Sew sleeve seams

Helpful Hints

When sewing up your seams, particularly if you are handsewing, use the same yarn you used to knit your project. If you don't have enough yarn, use a similar, finer yarn in a matching color. Don't go to your local five and dime and pick up a spool of sewing thread!

Before you begin seaming, you might consider basting the pieces together loosely. Basting is a sewing term used to indicate a stitch that isn't permanent. It holds the pieces together in the right position, so you can concentrate on the task of seaming, confident that you're doing it at the right place! You can also baste with pins.

Loose Ends: Let Me Fix My Weave

What to do with all the dangling threads? Once you've finished assembling your sweater, you're still not completely finished! You must weave in your ends. And for this you will need a tapestry needle—the kind of needle with a larger eye than you are accustomed to seeing on a sewing machine. Every project we work on will require the weaving in of ends. For the most part, you are starting with long tails.

To weave in ends, all you need to do is turn the work inside out and thread a tail onto your yarn needle. Insert the tip of the needle through a stitch—work toward the stitch that is a bar. Pull the needle and loose end through. And voilà—you've woven your first stitch. Repeat until you have woven your loose end through approximately five stitches. Snip off the remaining loose end. And finally, check your work on the Right Side to be certain none of the weave is poking through.

Helpful Hints

Don't start weaving in your ends until your project has been completely sewn together—the sleeves have been attached to the body, the fronts and backs have been sewn up, and so on. We wait until the end to weave to avoid creating bulky threaded areas.

Resist the temptation to pull the yarn through that first stitch super tight, as you don't want your work to fold in on itself. Keep the weave loose but secure.

Blocking

Many patterns will require blocking at the finishing stage. Blocking is a way of flattening the fabric to make it easier to seam. Of course, blocking is not just for seaming. It can open up lace patterns and be used to stretch out your piece if it is too small.

As with all knitting techniques, there are a number of ways to block. The Knitchicks prefer the steaming method. This requires an iron, ironing board (or other suitable surface) and a damp piece of cotton or linen fabric (clean teatowels work wonderfully).

Arrange the knitting on the ironing surface and then place a damp (not wet) piece of fabric directly on top of it. Lower the iron directly onto the cloth and hold it still—do not move the iron as you would when ironing regular clothes. You'll notice a lot of steam coming off the fabric as it dries out a bit. Pick up the iron and move it to a different part of the cloth and do the same again. When the fabric gets dry, wet and wring it out again. Please remember that you are not ironing your knitting—the iron must never move when in contact with the fabric!

PICKING UP STITCHES

Surprise! You will be picking up on the Right Side! Huh? Yes! When you pick up stitches, it leaves a telltale ridge on the opposite side of the fabric, like a seam. So, if you are working on the Right Side, the ridges will appear on the Wrong Side.

When you pick up stitches, you work straight across, from the Right Side, knitting into the selvedge (the side margins). If you're attaching a sleeve, the key is to make sure you have the same or close to the same number of stitches on the work you're attaching it to. However, collars generally require fewer stitches. Anything picked up in the round will be worked clockwise.

To pick up a stitch, insert your needle from the front as if to knit and shove it through both strands, or the V, of the stitch. Once your needle is inserted, then wrap your yarn as you would to knit, and knit away. This is called "pick up and knit" because you have not only put the new stitch on the needle (as in a cast on) but completed the first row of knitting. Don't panic if the math is off, or the stitches aren't matching up. You can fix this when you seam your edges.

The Handy Dandy Knitchicks' Chart

It may seem tedious to tear your fingers away from the knitting to take notes, but you'll be very happy you took the time to do it. With the Knitchicks' checklist, you'll be able to jot down all your pertinent info. Make photocopies of this list and use it for every project you take on!

PROJECT

Yarn I Am Using: _____

Number of Skeins: _____

Type of Fiber: _____

Label Care: _____

Test Swatch Results: _____

Gauge: _____

Needle(s) I Am Using: _____

Pattern I Am Using: _____

From What Book/Source: _____

I Cast On How Many Stitches: _____

Notes:

MEASUREMENTS

Torso: _____

Circumference of Neck: _____

Bust Width: _____

Waist Width: _____

Hips Width: _____

Length from Neck to Bottom: _____

Shoulder to Wrist: _____

Underarm to Wrist: _____

Circumference of Upper Arm: _____

Circumference of Wrist: _____

Armhole: _____

FINISHING

Seaming Technique Used: _____

Notes:

Me! Me! Me!

Patterns for Women

Truth be told, we knit for ourselves. That's right, we said it. The Knitchicks like to make garments we can wear ourselves. Oh, sure, we're happy to make items for loved ones and people we want to suck up to...but really? It's all about us. In this chapter, every top is something we've designed for ourselves. We hope you enjoy them as much as we do.

Our designs are created with an eye toward versatility—many of these pieces can easily be adjusted for your teenagers, your significant other and even your kids. It's a matter of adjusting the yarn color and playing with the measurements. As always, we encourage you to make your mark on all of these designs and make them your own.

Shula

I must confess: Somewhere along the line, when I wasn't looking, I gained weight and all my snug-fitting tops became ill fitting and unflattering. Uncomfortable in my new body, I started making things for myself that were loose and comfortable. Anything to numb the discomfort, anything that would be flattering to my new shape.

So I've made a comfortable roll-top sleeveless top. A project that's knit in the round with a slight detour to straight needles, this simple top is a quick knit. And here's a tip: The bulkier the yarn, the quicker the knitting will go. It's knit from the top down with only slight shaping—it was designed to hide the parts of me that were spilling over, after all.

Marcelle

FINISHED SIZES
Bust: 32–38 (40–46, 48+)" (81–97 [102–117, 122+]cm)
Length from Shoulder: 21" (53cm)

Note: See the pattern for instructions on customizing the sweater to fit your measurements and desired fit.

FIT
Classic

YARN
3 skeins Cascade Yarns Baby Alpaca Chunky (100% baby alpaca, 108yds [99m] per 100g skein)
color 568 Moss Green (MC)
1 skein Cascade Yarns Baby Alpaca Chunky (100% baby alpaca, 108yds [99m] per 100g skein)
color 553 Black (CC)

NEEDLES
16" and 32" (40cm and 80cm) size US 10 (6mm) circular needles
size US 10 (6mm) straight needles

NOTIONS
stitch marker
removable markers
tapestry needle

GAUGE
12 sts and 18 rows = 4" (10cm) in St st

NOTES

M1 (make 1): Inc 1 st by picking up the bar between the next st and the st just knit and knitting into it.

Sl marker or sl st(s) (slip marker or slip stitch[es]): Slip a st or sts purlwise from the left needle to the right needle. When slipping a marker, knit the sts before and after it as usual.

pm (place marker): Slip a premade marker or a loosely knotted piece of scrap yarn in a contrasting color onto the right needle after the stitch just knit to mark a spot in the knitting to refer to on future rows. When you come to a marker, simply slip it from the left-hand needle to the right-hand needle.

k2tog (knit 2 together): Dec 1 st by knitting 2 sts tog.

yo (yarn over): Wrap the working yarn around the needle, and work the next st as usual. This operation creates an eyelet hole in the knitting and inc 1 st.

SSK (slip, slip, knit): Dec 1 st by slipping 2 sts knitwise 1 at a time, inserting the tip of the left needle into both sts and knitting the 2 sts tog.

ROLL-TOP COWL

Beg with the shorter circular needle and MC, CO 60 (64, 68) sts. Join for working in the rnd, pm at the beg of the rnd, and another at the halfway point of the rnd (after 30 [32, 34] sts).

Work in St st for about 2" (5cm), or 3" (8cm) if you want a nice chunky roll top.

This top is knit from the top down with minimal shaping.

You can cast on more stitches if you want a more dramatic cowl neck, or fewer for a closer-fitting funnel neck.

INCREASE FOR SHOULDERS

Once your neck is nice and roll-y, begin increasing for the shoulders. Inc 1 st before and after each marker on every second rnd until you have approx 92 (100, 108) sts. Inc using the make 1 method as foll: Knit to marker, M1, sl marker, k1, M1.

You may prefer a few stitches more or less at this point, depending on the width of your shoulders. Here's a tip: Your armholes will roll naturally inward, making a really nice edge finish. So you don't need to knit a fancy border.

SEPARATE FOR FRONT AND BACK

Now you need to work the front and back of your top, independently of one another. Let's work on the front portion first. Pull out your straight needles and knit across half of the sts, from one marker to the other. Leave the other half on the circular. You'll get to it soon enough.

Cont in St st, inc 1 st at each end of approx every 4th row, until you have half the total bust sts needed for your size. Smaller sizes (finished bust 42" [107cm] and under) should work inc every 4th row. Mid-range sizes (44"–50" [112–127cm]) will probably do best with a mix: Alternate inc on every 2nd row and every 4th row. Larger sizes might want to inc every 2nd row only. Work the front in this manner until it is long enough to reach from the top of your shoulder to the underarm. Set the front aside, and with a new ball of yarn, work the back, which is resting on your circular needles. Knit the back the same as the front.

Slip the first stitch of every row for neat edges.

In this section, your goal is to increase to the total number of stitches needed for your finished bust size. Half the increases will be on the front section, and half on the back. In order to get the right number of stitches without making the armholes too short or too long, different sizes will need to increase at different rates. The best-fitting rate of increase depends on your individual shoulder width, bust size and armhole depth, so measure, measure, measure and try on often!

It's easiest if you always work your increases on Right Side (knit) rows.

JOIN TO WORK DOWN FROM UNDERARMS

Once the front and back are done, knit all the sts onto the longer circular needle. Pm at each underarm. The sample top has a simple eyelet pattern at each side of the waist. To add this detail to your top, on every 4th rnd work as foll: *Knit to 2 sts before marker, k2tog, yo, k1, sl marker, k1, yo, SSK; rep from * once more.

Work even in St st in the rnd until you reach your desired length, minus 1½" (4cm) for the border.

GARTER STITCH HEM

When you've gotten to your desired length, switch to CC. This will be your garter st border. I really like the way the garter border lies at the bottom of a top. It has a classy look to it. To do garter st in the rnd, you knit 1 rnd, you purl the next. Go figure.

Knit until the border is approx 1½" (4cm) thick.

Bind off very loosely.

Things to think about: As you knit your body, think about how long you want it to be. I've knit this one to fall just below my belly button, but some people will want it longer.

approx. 20 (21½, 22½)"
(51 [55, 57]cm)

length from top of your shoulder to the underarm

your shoulder width + approx. 2" (5cm)

length from underarm to just below belly button, or longer

your bust measurement + 2" (5cm)

Friendly Reminder
Measure yourself! Measure the width of your shoulders, measure from your shoulder to underarm. As for the length of this top, that can be as long or short as you please!

Jess

I avoided knitting tops for a very long time because I was intimidated by keeping track of the number of rows I knit. How would I knit the same amount of rows for the front and for the back? I gravitated to knitting in the round because it didn't require much keeping track. Finally, a wise knitter—my Mom—told me the way to keep track was to take notes. (Why didn't I think of that?) So I started writing down row counts, where I was and what I was doing. Keeping copious notes helped me overcome what had kept me from pursuing knitting tops.

These days I use homemade journals—those notebooks you find in bookstores—and customize them to my knitting note needs. I like working with graph papers and using the little boxes to represent numbers and rows. Now I knit merrily along with the confidence that I am not losing count and that my sides will meet as they need to.

I designed Jess because I decided that I wanted an easy-to-knit warm weather top. Fixation is a fabulous yarn to knit with as it is elastic—it stretches along with you!

Marcelle

FINISHED MEASUREMENTS

Measure your bust and subtract 1–2" (3–5cm) for negative ease. For example, the sample as shown was knit for a woman's size Small.
Sample measurements:
Bust: 32" (82cm)
Length from shoulder: 20" (51cm)

FIT

Very close

YARN

sample shown uses 5 skeins Cascade Yarns Fixation (98.3% cotton, 1.7% elastic; 100 yds (91m) per 50g skein)

color #9226 variegated red

NEEDLES

29" (74cm) size US 5 (3.75mm) circular needle

NOTIONS

row counter (optional)
crochet hook (optional)
stitch markers
tapestry needle

GAUGE

25 sts and 39 rows = 4" (10cm) in St st

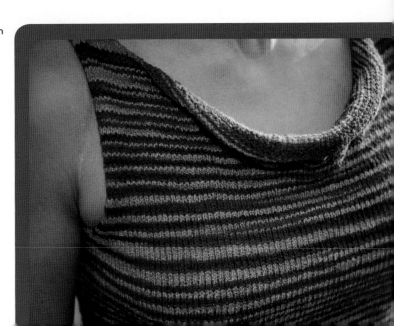

NOTES

k2tog (knit 2 together): Dec 1 st by knitting 2 sts tog.

pm (place marker): Slip a premade marker or a loosely knotted piece of scrap yarn in a contrasting color onto the right needle after the stitch just knit to mark a spot in the knitting to refer to on future rows. When you come to a marker, simply slip it from the left-hand needle to the right-hand needle.

Sl marker or sl st(s) (slip marker or slip stitch[es]): Slip a st or sts purlwise from the left needle to the right needle. When slipping a marker, knit the sts before and after it as usual.

SSK (slip, slip, knit): Dec 1 st by slipping 2 sts knitwise 1 at a time, inserting the tip of the left needle into both sts and knitting the 2 sts tog.

M1 (make 1): Inc 1 st by picking up the bar between the next st and the st just knit and knitting into it.

HEM

CO the number of sts required for your bust size minus 1–2" (3–5cm) for negative ease. The sample shown starts with 200 sts. Join for knitting in the rnd.

Pm at the beg of the rnd and at the halfway point of the rnd.

*Knit 1 row. Purl 1 row. Rep from * 3 times more.

This top should fit snugly, with at least 1" (3cm) of negative ease. Round your cast-on number up to the nearest even number.

These rows create a garter stitch border. To knit garter stitch in the round, knit one row, purl the next.

BODY

Once you've got your hem, you head into the body of the piece. For the body, knit in the rnd for 13½" (34cm).

Measure yourself from the bottom of your armpit to the point where your hip bone juts out to determine if you need to knit a bit longer than 13½" (34cm).

SEPARATE FOR FRONT AND BACK

Let's work the back panel first. On the RS, bind off 5 sts. Work to the second stitch marker. Turn your piece and begin a purl row. Bind off 5 sts and purl to end.

The beauty of working on a circular needle is that you can keep the panel-in-waiting on the needle.

Shape Back Armholes

Next Row (RS): K1, SSK, k to last 3 sts, k2tog, k1—2 sts dec.

Next Row (WS): Purl.

Rep these 2 rows until you reach the desired cross-back width. Write down how many sts are left on your needle so you can duplicate this shaping on the front.

Work even in St st until desired armhole depth, less 1" (3cm).

How do you find your cross-back width? Stand up straight and have a friend measure across your shoulders from the outside of one bra strap to the outside of the other. Add 1" (3cm) to this measurement to get the cross-back width.

Shape Back Neck

On the next RS row, k12 sts, join a second ball of yarn, BO until there are 12 sts left at the end of the row, knit to the end.

Work even on each set of 12 sts, using separate balls of yarn, for 1" (3cm). BO all sts.

To find the armhole depth, either measure a tank top that fits you well, in a straight line from the shoulder to the underarm, or have someone measure your back straight down from the shoulder to the underarm.

This leaves you with 12 sts for each shoulder, a narrow strap. Adjust the straps by binding off more or fewer stitches for the back neck. If you change the shoulder width on the back, remember to do the same on the front!

Shape Front Armholes

Join yarn to the other half of the sts rem on the needle, with the RS facing. Bind off 5 sts, knit to end. Turn, bind off 5 sts, purl to end.

NEXT ROW (RS): K1, SSK, k to last 3 sts, k2tog, k1—2 sts dec.

NEXT ROW (WS): Purl.

Rep these 2 rows until sts equal same as back.

Shape the front armholes the same as the back.

Shape Front Neck

Pm for cowl neck inc at 4 points along neckline as foll: Find the center front of your top. Count 6 sts to either side of center front and pm at each spot to mark center 12 sts. We'll call these the A markers.

Now count 12 sts to either side of the A markers and pm of a different color at each spot. We'll call these the B markers. A total of 36 center front sts are marked off.

If the marker placement isn't clear to you, take a look at the schematic. Each of the radiating lines on the front neck represents a line of increases. That's where your markers should be.

Cowl Increases

NEXT RS ROW: Knit to first A marker, sl marker, M1, knit to second A marker, M1, sl marker, k to end—2 sts inc.

Work 3 rows even.

This first set of increases is worked at the A markers only.

NEXT ROW (RS): Knit to first B marker, sl marker, M1, knit to first A marker, sl marker, M1, knit to second A marker, M1, sl marker, knit to second B marker, M1, sl marker, k to end—4 sts inc.

Work 5 rows even.

Now you'll begin increasing at all 4 markers.

Rep these 6 rows until desired armhole depth less 1½" (4cm).

If you don't end with a perfect repeat of 6 rows here, that's fine! Just go on to the next step when the armhole depth is right.

Shape Shoulders

NEXT RS ROW: K15, BO until 15 sts rem at end of the row, knit to end.

Working on the right shoulder only, purl 1 WS row.

If you changed the number of shoulder/strap stitches on the back, adjust it here as well. You want to have the back shoulder stitch count + 3 at this stage.

NEXT ROW (RS): K1, SSK, knit to end—1 st dec.

Rep last 2 rows twice more, for a total of 3 sts dec.

Work even on rem sts until armhole measures same as back to shoulder. BO.

Left Shoulder

Rejoin yarn to left shoulder with WS facing. Purl 1 WS row.

NEXT ROW (RS): Knit to last 3 sts, k2tog, k1—1 st dec.

Rep last 2 rows twice more, for a total of 3 sts dec.

Work even on rem sts until armhole measures same as back to shoulder. BO.

FINISHING

Seam shoulders. Weave in ends. The armholes and neck of this top will naturally curl. If you want them to lie flat, work a row of single crochet around the edges.

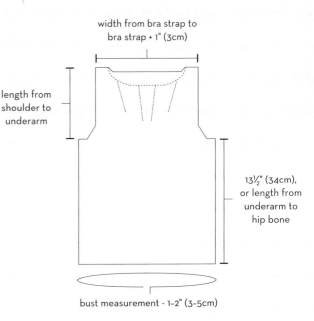

width from bra strap to bra strap + 1" (3cm)

length from shoulder to underarm

13½" (34cm), or length from underarm to hip bone

bust measurement - 1–2" (3–5cm)

Allez Hélène

My friend Helen always found the air conditioning in her office insufficient, so she asked me to design her a vest (called a sleeveless jumper or bodywarmer in the United Kingdom). The result is a diamond pattern created by ribbing. As is the Knitchicks' fancy, this top is knit in the round. Because it's ribbed, the piece looks quite small when laid flat, but when worn, the diamonds are in their element.

Pauline

FINISHED MEASUREMENTS
Bust (unstretched): 26 (31, 36, 41)" (66 [79, 91, 104]cm)
Length (unstretched): 23¾ (24, 24¼, 24½)" (60 [61, 62, 62]cm)

FIT
Very close (at least 2" [5cm] negative ease)

YARN
5 (7, 8, 9) skeins RYC Bamboo Soft (100% bamboo, 112yds [102m] per 50g skein)
color 110 Pompadour

NEEDLES
24" (60cm) size US 6 (4mm) circular needle

NOTIONS
stitch marker
stitch holders
tapestry needle

GAUGE
28 sts and 32 rows = 4" (10cm) in chart pattern, measured unstretched
36 sts and 28 rows = 4" (10cm) in k1, p1 rib, measured unstretched

NOTES

pm (place marker): Slip a premade marker or a loosely knotted piece of scrap yarn in a contrasting color onto the right needle after the stitch just knit to mark a spot in the knitting to refer to on future rows. When you come to a marker, simply slip it from the left-hand needle to the right-hand needle.

Sl marker or sl st(s) (slip marker or slip stitch[es]): Slip a st or sts purlwise from the left needle to the right needle. When slipping a marker, knit the sts before and after it as usual.

K2tog (knit 2 together): Dec 1 st by knitting 2 sts tog.

p2tog (purl 2 together): Dec 1 st by purling 2 sts tog.

p2tog tbl (purl 2 together through back loop): Dec 1 st by inserting the needle into the backs of the next 2 sts and purling them tog.

SSK (slip, slip, knit): Dec 1 st by slipping 2 sts knitwise 1 at a time, inserting the tip of the left needle into both sts and knitting the 2 sts tog.

BODY

CO 180 (216, 252, 288) sts using the cable cast-on method. (For a challenge you could try the more difficult, but ultra-neat, tubular cast-on method.)

Pm and join for working in the rnd.

RNDS 1–4: *P1, k1; rep from * to end.

Work Rnds 1–24 of Diamonds Chart 4 times, then Rnds 1–13 once more. Work Rnd 14, ending this rnd 5 (7, 9, 11) sts before the marker.

SEPARATE FOR FRONT AND BACK

BO 11 (13, 17, 21) sts, work in patt until you have 79 (95, 109, 123) sts on right-hand needle, BO 11 (13, 17, 21) sts, work in patt to end.

You now have 2 sets of 79 (95, 109, 123) sts each.

UPPER BACK

Size 26 only:

NEXT ROW (WS): Sl 1, work in patt to end.

NEXT ROW (RS): Sl 1, p1, SSK, work in patt to last 4 sts, k2tog, p1, k1—2 sts dec.

Rep last 2 rows 4 times more—69 sts.

NEXT ROW (WS): Sl 1, k1, work in patt to last 2 sts, k1, p1.

Size 31 only:

NEXT ROW (WS): Sl 1, k1, p2tog, work in patt to last 4 sts, p2tog tbl, k1, p1—2 sts dec.

NEXT ROW (RS): Sl 1, p1, SSK, work in patt to last 4 sts, k2tog, p1, k1—2 sts dec.

Rep last 2 rows 3 times more—79 sts.

NEXT ROW (WS): Sl 1, k1, work in patt to last 2 sts, k1, p1.

NEXT ROW (RS): Sl 1, p1, SSK, work in patt to last 4 sts, k2tog, p1, k1—2 sts dec—77 sts.

NEXT ROW (WS): Sl 1, k1, work in patt to last 2 sts, k1, p1.

If you want to increase the length of the garment, it must be done in 24-round increments (a full pattern repeat).

Diamonds Chart

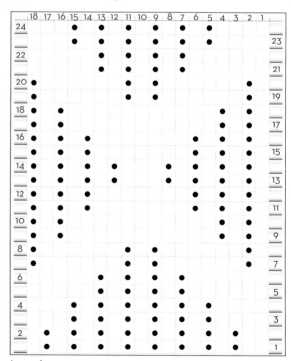

Legend

☐ Knit

● Purl

Sizes 36 (41) only:

NEXT ROW (WS): Sl 1, k1, p2tog, work in patt to last 4 sts, p2tog tbl, k1, p1—2 sts dec.

NEXT ROW (RS): Sl 1, p1, SSK, work in patt to last 4 sts, k2tog, p1, k1—2 sts dec.

Rep last 2 rows 4 times more, then WS row only once—87 (101) sts.

**All sizes:

NEXT ROW (RS): Sl 1, *p1, k1; rep from * to end.

NEXT ROW (WS): Sl 1, *k1, p1; rep from * to end.

Cont in rib as set by last 2 rows until armhole measures 8¼ (8, 8, 7¼)" (21 [20, 20, 18]cm) (measured unstretched), ending with a WS row.

Shape Neck

NEXT ROW (RS): Sl 1, work 33 (38, 42, 49) sts in rib, BO 1 st, sl 1, SSK, work in rib to end.

Left Shoulder

NEXT ROW (WS): Sl 1, work in rib to last 3 sts, p2tog tbl, p1.

NEXT ROW (RS): Sl 1, SSK, work in rib to end.

Rep last 2 rows until 26 (29, 32, 35) sts rem. Place sts on holder.

Right Shoulder

Join yarn with WS facing.

NEXT ROW (WS): Sl 1, p2tog, work in rib to end.

NEXT ROW (RS): Sl 1, work in rib to last 3 sts, k2tog, k1.

Rep last 2 rows until 26 (29, 32, 35) sts rem. Place sts on holder.

UPPER FRONT

Work as for upper back to **.

NEXT ROW (RS): Sl 1, *p1, k1; rep from * to end.

NEXT ROW (WS): Sl 1, *k1, p1; rep from * to end.

Divide for V-Neck

NEXT ROW (RS): Sl 1, work 33 (38, 42, 49) sts in rib, BO 1 st, work in rib to end.

The V-neck will now be worked in two pieces. You can place the first set of stitches onto a holder, or because you are working on a circular needle, just leave it be and "ignore."

Right Shoulder

NEXT ROW (WS): Sl 1, work in rib to last 3 sts, p2tog tbl, p1.

NEXT ROW (RS): Sl 1, work in rib to end.

Rep last 2 rows until 26 (29, 32, 35) sts rem.

NEXT ROW (WS): Sl 1, work in rib to end.

NEXT ROW (RS): Sl 1, work in rib to end.

Rep last 2 rows until front measures same as back to shoulder. Place sts on holder.

Left Shoulder

Join yarn with WS facing.

NEXT ROW (WS): Sl 1, p2tog, work in rib to end.

NEXT ROW (RS): Sl 1, work in rib to end.

Rep last 2 rows until 26 (29, 32, 35) sts rem.

NEXT ROW (WS): Sl 1, work in rib to end.

NEXT ROW (RS): Sl 1, work in rib to end.

Rep last 2 rows until front measures same as back to shoulder.

FINISHING

There will be 4 sets of live sts. Use the 3-needle bind-off method to create shoulder seams.

Alternately, for a more challenging but neater and seamless finish, graft the pieces using Kitchener stitch (see pages 32–33).

Weave in ends.

7½ (8½, 9½, 11)"
(19 [22, 24, 28]cm)

14" (36cm)

9¾ (10, 10¼, 10½)"
(25 [25, 26, 27]cm)

26 (31, 36, 41)"
(66 [79, 91, 104]cm)

Why not try the piece on? Be careful not to stab yourself with needles or let any stitches fall off. Stretch the straps up to your shoulder (it will stretch naturally when finished) to determine whether or not you like the fit.

Isla

Isla is from the fair isle of Argyll (get it?). Working with two colors and stranding the unused color across the back is known as fair isle. This simple argyle pattern is an easy way to cut your teeth on a new technique. On such big needles and with chunky yarn, you'll get to show off your newfound skill quickly!

Pauline

FINISHED SIZES
Bust: 31–35 (37–41, 43–47, 49+)" (79–89 [94–104, 109–119, 125+]cm)
Length from Shoulder: 22" (56cm)

Note: See the pattern for instructions on customizing the sweater to fit your measurements and desired fit.

FIT
Classic

YARN
4 balls of Rowan Big Wool (100% merino wool, 87yds [80m] per 100g ball)
    Color 026 Blue Velvet (MC)
1 ball of Rowan Big Wool in each of the following colors:
    Color 037 Zing (CC1)
    Color 038 Flirty (CC2)

NEEDLES
size US 17 (12mm) straight needles

NOTIONS
bobbins (optional)
tapestry needle

GAUGE
8 sts and 11 rows = 4" (10cm) in St st

NOTES

k2tog (knit 2 together): Dec 1 st by knitting 2 sts tog.

SSK (slip, slip, knit): Dec 1 st by slipping 2 sts knitwise 1 at a time, inserting the tip of the left needle into both sts and knitting the 2 sts tog.

FRONT/BACK (MAKE 2 ALIKE)

With MC, CO the number of sts needed for your bust measurement divided by 2, plus 2 sts for selvedges.

Knit 1 row. Purl 1 row.

Work the 15 rows of the Argyle Chart with CC1 and CC2 (1 color on the front and the other on the back), ending with an RS row.

Work even in St st until piece measures 12½" (32cm) or desired length to underarm, ending with a WS row.

BO 3 sts at beg of next 2 rows.

Work even until armholes measure your armhole depth plus 1" (3cm), ending with a WS row.

BO 3 (4, 5, 6) sts at beg of next 4 rows.

Work 3 more rows over rem sts, ending with an RS row.

BO knitwise on WS very loosely.

SLEEVES (MAKE 2 ALIKE)

Using MC, with RS facing, beg at underarm pick up and knit 1 st in each st at base of armhole and 2 sts for every 3 rows around armhole.

Work in St st, dec 1 st at each end of the 6th row, then every foll 10th row 3 times.

Work even until sleeve measures 19" (48cm), or desired length from underarm.

BO loosely.

FINISHING

Block all the pieces. Use mattress stitch (see page 32) to seam neck and shoulders. Sew side and sleeve seams with mattress st.

Your cast-on stitches should be rounded to the nearest odd number. You'll need an odd number of stitches to center the argyle pattern.

The pattern is worked using a stranded colorwork technique, in different colors on the back and front. To center the argyle pattern, find the center stitch of your work and match it to the center stitch on the chart. Count to the right on the chart to find the correct starting place for your size. The chart is read bottom to top, right to left on RS (odd numbered) rows, and left to right on WS (even numbered) rows.

This is the base of the armholes. Your armhole depth is measured from the top of your shoulder straight down to underarm level. I added 1" (3cm) for ease.

This is the shoulder shaping.
For a higher neck, work an extra 2 rows here.

These square set-in sleeves are worked from the top down. Tip: Leave yarn tails long enough to seam the neck and shoulders.

Larger sizes may want to decrease more sts, more often—perhaps every 8th row 4 times.

Use a combination of k2tog and SSK for your decreases. We call these "directional decreases" because the k2tog decrease leans to the right, and the SSK decrease leans to the left. When combined, the decreases create pleasing diagonal lines that mirror the edge of the fabric. In this case, you should decrease with SSK on the right side of each row and with k2tog on the left side of each row.

It is important in this pattern to block the pieces. Blocking serves two purposes: flattening the hem, which by now will probably be rolling (as Stockinette stitch does), and also making the edges easier to see and therefore sew up. To block, we recommend placing a clean, damp tea towel over each piece and steaming with an iron.

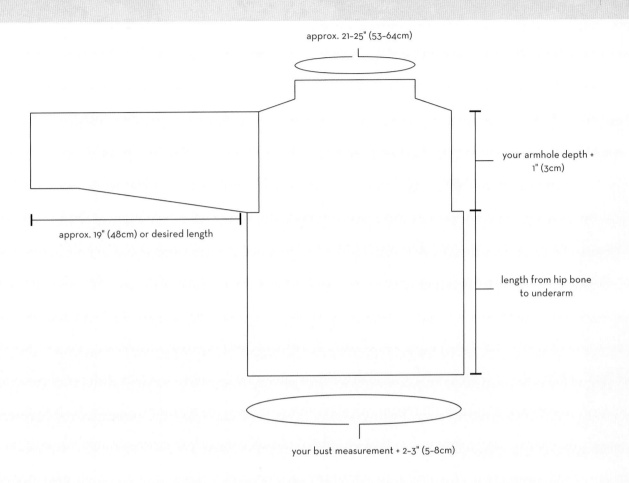

approx. 21–25" (53–64cm)

your armhole depth +
1" (3cm)

approx. 19" (48cm) or desired length

length from hip bone
to underarm

your bust measurement + 2–3" (5–8cm)

Argyle Chart

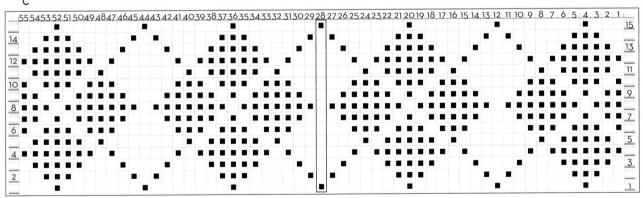

Legend

☐ Knit

■ Color 1

Notes: Bordered stitch (#28) is center stitch.

Marcelle

Sometimes it's a particular yarn that inspires me to create a design. When I first saw the Tilli Tomas yarn sitting in Knitty City, my LYS, I thought, dang, I need to make something sultry and sexy for myself with this yarn. After consulting my closet I came up with the Marcelle, a romantic number I can wear to the office and then later to a candlelit dinner with my Honey.

This top is knit in the round from the bottom up. The body and sleeves are first worked separately, then they are united on a circular needle and worked with raglan shaping to the collar. A keyhole at the front of the sweater creates a sexy peek-a-boo cutout. And the eyelets sprinkled throughout allow you to wear this top with or without a camisole underneath.

Marcelle

FINISHED MEASUREMENTS

Bust: 33½ (36, 38½, 41, 43)" (85 [91, 98, 104, 109]cm)
Length: 24¾ (25¼, 25¾, 26, 26¼)" (63 [64, 65, 66, 67]cm)

FIT

Close

YARN

7 (8, 9, 10, 10) skeins Tilli Tomas Plié (100% silk; 140yds [128m] per 50g skein)

color 180 Ruby Wine (MC)

2 (1, 1, 2, 2) skeins Tilli Tomas Beaded Plié (100% silk with beads; 140yds [128m] per 50g skein)

color 180 Ruby Wine (CC)

NEEDLES

24" (60cm) size US 7 (4.5mm) circular needle
size US 7 (4.5mm) DPNs

NOTIONS

stitch markers
stitch holders
crochet hook

GAUGE

20 sts and 28 rows = 4" (10cm) in St st

NOTES

k2tog (knit 2 together): Dec 1 st by knitting 2 sts tog.

yo (yarn over): Wrap the working yarn around the needle, and work the next st as usual. This operation creates an eyelet hole in the knitting and inc 1 st.

pm (place marker): Slip a premade marker or a loosely knotted piece of scrap yarn in a contrasting color onto the right needle after the stitch just knit to mark a spot in the knitting to refer to on future rows. When you come to a marker, simply slip it from the left-hand needle to the right-hand needle.

Sl marker or sl st(s) (slip marker or slip stitch[es]): Slip a st or sts purlwise from the left needle to the right needle. When slipping a marker, knit the sts before and after it as usual.

SSK (slip, slip, knit): Dec 1 st by slipping 2 sts knitwise 1 at a time, inserting the tip of the left needle into both sts and knitting the 2 sts tog.

M1L (make 1 left): Inc 1 st by lifting the bar between the st just knit and the next st onto the left-hand needle and knitting it through the back loop to prevent creating a hole in the knitted fabric.

BODY

Note: Throughout the body, alternate MC and CC as desired. The top will be very heavy if you use a lot of beaded yarn, so use a light hand with the CC.

With circular needle and MC, CO 168 (180, 192, 204, 216) sts. Pm and join for working in the rnd.

RND 1: *K2, p2; rep from * to end.

Rep Rnd 1 3 times more.

Work Rnds 1–44 of Lace Motif twice, then Rnds 1–22 again. Body should measure approx 16" (41cm) from cast-on edge.

Knit 1 rnd, ending this rnd 8 (9, 10, 11, 12) sts before the marker. Do not cut yarn. Place next 16 (18, 20, 22, 24) sts on holder for underarm. Set Body aside.

SLEEVES

Cuff

With DPNs and MC, CO 60 (65, 65, 72, 72) sts. Pm and join for working in the rnd.

RND 1: *K4 (5, 5, 4, 4), [k2tog, yo] 4 times; rep from * to end.

RND 2: Knit.

Rep Rnds 1–2 until cuff measures 3" (8cm) from cast-on edge.

Beg working in St st. Dec 1 st on every 3rd rnd 8 times by k2tog at beg of rnd—52 (57, 57, 64, 64) sts.

Change to CC. Dec 1 st on every 5th rnd 3 times by k2tog at beg of rnd—49 (54, 54, 61, 61) sts rem.

Work even until sleeve measures 11 (11, 11, 11½, 11½)" (28 [28, 29, 29, 29]cm) from cast-on edge.

Change to MC. Inc 1 st on every 3rd rnd 11 (10, 14, 11, 13) times by M1L at beg of rnd—60 (64, 68, 72, 74) sts.

The body is knit with a mix of beaded (CC) and plain (MC) Tili Tomas yarn.

The pattern is repetitive; however, you may decide the eyelets are a bit too revealing and forego all the yarn overs. You won't lose all the sexiness of the sweater even if you do leave out the eyelets. This yarn takes sexy to a whole new level.

You are decreasing to make the sleeve snug. When you get to the belled part of the sleeve, the snugness of the top will make the flare even more dramatic!

Lace Motif

Legend

☐	Knit	O	yo
●	Purl	\	ssk
/	k2tog		

Work even until sleeve measures 17½ (18, 18, 18½, 18½)" (45[46, 46, 47, 47]cm) from cast-on edge. End last rnd 8 (9, 10, 11, 12) sts before the marker. Place next 16 (18, 20, 22, 24) sts on holder for underarm. Cut yarn, leaving a long tail for grafting underarms later—44 (46, 48, 50, 50) sts rem.

YOKE

Unite body and sleeves on circular needle as foll:

With circular needle holding body sts, pm, knit across sts of 1 sleeve, pm, knit across 68 (72, 76, 80, 84) body sts, place next 16 (18, 20, 22, 24) body sts on holder for underarm, pm, knit across sts of second sleeve, pm, k 34 (36, 38, 40, 42) body sts, pm for beg of rnd. Beg of rnd is located at center back—224 (236, 248, 260, 268) sts.

Raglan Shaping

Knit 3 rnds.

NEXT RND: *Knit to 2 sts before marker, k2tog, sl marker, k2tog; rep from * 3 times more, knit to end of rnd—8 sts dec.

Rep these 4 rnds 3 times more—192 (204, 216, 228, 236) sts.

Knit 2 rnds.

Front Neck Shaping

At end of last rnd, remove beg-of-rnd marker and turn work.

Purl 1 WS row.

NEXT ROW (RS): SSK, *knit to 2 sts before marker, k2tog, sl marker, k2tog; rep from * 3 times more, knit to last 2 sts, k2tog—10 sts dec.

Rep these 2 rows 7 (7, 8, 8, 8) times more—112 (124, 126, 138, 146) sts.

Purl 1 WS row.

NEXT ROW (RS): *Knit to 2 sts before marker, k2tog, sl marker, k2tog; rep from * 3 times more, knit to end—8 sts dec.

Rep these 2 rows 6 (7, 7, 8, 9) times more—56 (60, 62, 66, 66) sts.

Choker Collar

At the end of last RS row, do not turn. Use backward-loop method (see page 19) or cable method (see page 23) to CO 22 (22, 22, 22, 22) sts, pm and join for working in the rnd.

Knit 1 rnd.

Change to CC and work in garter st (p 1 rnd, k 1 rnd) for 1" (3cm).

Bind off.

FINISHING

Seam the underarms using Kitchener stitch (see pages 32–33) and the yarn tails from sleeves.

With MC, work 1 row of single crochet around the back opening.

Weave in ends.

Be sure to posititon the sleeve so it matches the stitches at the bottom part of the sleeve.

This is where you join the sleeves to the body. When you add the sleeves, you will be adding more stitches to the body.

When you begin the raglan shaping, you will decrease to compensate for the added stitches.

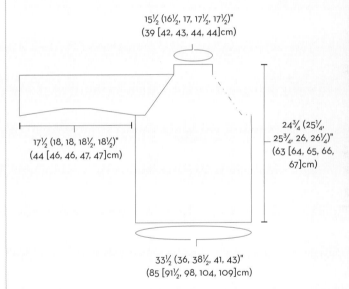

15½ (16½, 17, 17½, 17½)"
(39 [42, 43, 44, 44]cm)

24¾ (25¼, 25¾, 26, 26¼)"
(63 [64, 65, 66, 67]cm)

17½ (18, 18, 18½, 18½)"
(44 [46, 46, 47, 47]cm)

33½ (36, 38½, 41, 43)"
(85 [91½, 98, 104, 109]cm)

Morgan

I've always loved that casual 1970s style of clothing—the way you could lace a shirt up and still look sexy. That easy feeling was my thinking behind this top. I wanted to incorporate a 1970s vibe into a basic winter top I could wear to the office. I designed this top for a woman, but I also included notes on knitting it for a child, male or female. The only adjustment required is a change in yarn and color scheme.

Marcelle

FINISHED MEASUREMENTS

Measure your chest and add 1–2" (3–5cm) for ease.
For example, the sample as shown was knit for a petite adult woman (about a size 4 or 6).
Sample measurements:
Bust: 34" (86cm)
Length: 20" (51cm)

FIT
Close

YARN

6 skeins Karabella Yarns Aurora 8 (100% extrafine merino wool, 98yds [90m] per 50g skein)
color 6 brown (MC)
1 skein Karabella Yarns Aurora 8 (100% extrafine merino wool, 98yds [90m] per 50g skein)
color 1530 purple (CC)

NEEDLES

32" (80cm) size US 9 (5.5mm) circular needle
size US 9 (5.5mm) DPNs

NOTIONS

stitch markers
stitch holders
crochet hook

GAUGE

13 sts and 19 rows = 4" (10cm) in St st

NOTES

pm (place marker): Slip a premade marker or a loosely knotted piece of scrap yarn in a contrasting color onto the right needle after the stitch just knit to mark a spot in the knitting to refer to on future rows. When you come to a marker, simply slip it from the left-hand needle to the right-hand needle.

yo (yarn over): Wrap the working yarn around the needle, and knit the next st as usual. This operation creates an eyelet hole in the knitting and inc 1 st.

Sl marker or sl st(s) (slip marker or slip stitch[es]): Slip a st or sts purlwise from the left needle to the right needle. When slipping a marker, knit the sts before and after it as usual.

k2tog (knit 2 together): Dec 1 st by knitting 2 sts tog.

KFB: Inc 1 st by knitting into the next st, and without sliding the st off the left-hand needle, knitting into the back of the same st. Slide old st off left-hand needle, creating 2 new sts on right-hand needle.

YOKE

With circular needle and MC, CO enough sts to fit comfortably around your neck. The sample shown starts with 54 sts. Do not join.

Knit 2 rows.

SET-UP ROW: Knit ⅓ of sts, pm for front sts; knit half of the next ⅓ of sts, pm for left sleeve; knit ⅓ of sts, pm for back; knit rem sleeve sts, place unique marker for beg of rnd.

BODY

Raglan Shaping

Now you'll work the raglan inc. At the same time, you'll knit eyelets into each front edge to run the lacing through later.

ROW 1 (RS): K2, yo, k2tog, *knit to 1 st before marker, KFB, sl marker, KFB; rep from * 3 times more, knit to last 4 sts, k2tog, yo, k2—8 sts inc.

ROWS 2, 4 AND 6 (WS): K4, purl to last 4 sts, k4.

ROWS 3 AND 5: *Knit to 1 st before marker, KFB, sl marker, KFB; rep from * 3 times more, knit to end.

Rep Rows 1–6 until the number of sts in the front and back sections tog equal the number of sts needed for desired bust measurement. End with a RS row.

At the end of the last row, do not turn. Join for working in the rnd.

Knit 1 rnd with MC. Change to CC and knit 1 rnd.

If you're a tight knitter, try to cast on as loosely as possible. For an open neck like this, you want as much give as possible.

You are casting on a small amount of stitches as you are creating an open, plunging V neck and will rapidly increase as you form your raglan sleeves.

The first part of the sweater is knit back-and-forth in Stockinette, without joining.

Raglan sweaters follow the rule of thirds: ⅓ of your sts are devoted to the front part of the sweater; ⅓ of your sts are devoted to the back of the sweater; ⅓ of your sts are for the sleeves, and you divide that final third by 2.

You'll place your stitch markers using this rule.

For a CO of 54 sts, it looks like this: K9 (Right Front), k9 (Right Sleeve), k18 (Back), k9 (Left Sleeve), k9 (Left Front).

Separate Sleeves and Body

On the next rnd, separate the sleeves from the body as foll: *Knit to marker, remove marker, place all sleeve sts on a holder, remove next marker; rep from * once more, knit to end of rnd.

All the body sts are now on the circular needle.

Pm and consider this the beg of the rnd from now on.

Change back to MC and knit 2 rnds.

Ribbing

NEXT RND: *K5, p1; rep from * to end.

Rep this rnd until sweater measures about 19¼" (49cm) from shoulder, or desired length less ¾" (2cm).

Change to CC and work in garter st for 4 rnds.

BO loosely.

SLEEVES (MAKE 2)

Place the held sleeve sts on DPNs. Join for working in the rnd.

Knit 2 rnds with CC. Change to MC and work even in St st for 5" (13cm), or desired length.

Change to CC and work 6 rnds garter st.

BO loosely.

FINISHING

Cord

Pick up your trusty crochet hook and MC, and chain for approx 30" (76cm). Lace the cord through the eyelets.

Weave in ends.

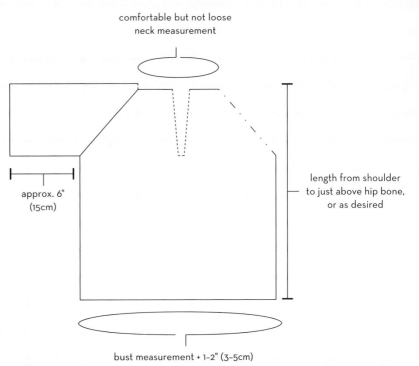

comfortable but not loose neck measurement

approx. 6" (15cm)

length from shoulder to just above hip bone, or as desired

bust measurement + 1–2" (3–5cm)

Mini Morgan

While I designed the Morgan for an adult, it occurred to me that a child—male or female—could sport this top as well. So I modified the measurements (making it much more loose fitting around the torso), switched up the yarn (using the lightweight Malabrigo and Organik), and added a few other touches to it. You can also knit this in a lightweight cotton for all-season wear.

Marcelle

FINISHED MEASUREMENTS

Measure the child's chest and add 4–6" (10–15cm) for ease.
For example, the sample as shown was knit for an 8-year-old child.
Sample measurements:
Chest: 41" (104cm)
Length: 17½" (45cm)

FIT

Very loose

YARN

2 skeins The Fibre Company Organik (70% merino wool, 15% baby alpaca, 15% silk, 85yds [78m] per 50g skein)
　　　color Sea Green (A)
1 skein The Fibre Company Organik (70% merino wool, 15% baby alpaca, 15% silk, 85yds [78m] per 50g skein)
　　　color Salmon (B)
2 skeins Malabrigo Yarn Chunky (100% merino wool, 104yds [95m] per 100g skein)
　　　color Azul Profundo (C)

Note: In the sweater shown, the bottom ribbed portion is knit with a heavier yarn at a larger gauge than the top. This helps to create the flared bottom, but you can use the same weight yarn for both parts to good effect.

NEEDLES

16" and 24" (40cm and 60cm) size US 9 (5.5mm) circular needles

NOTIONS

stitch markers
stitch holders
crochet hook

GAUGE

16 sts and 22 rows = 4" (10cm) in St st with color A
14 sts and 21 rows = 4" (10cm) in k6, p1 rib with color C

NOTES

pm (place marker): Slip a premade marker or a loosely knotted piece of scrap yarn in a contrasting color onto the right needle after the stitch just knit to mark a spot in the knitting to refer to on future rows. When you come to a marker, simply slip it from the left-hand needle to the right-hand needle.

yo (yarn over): Wrap the working yarn around the needle, and knit the next st as usual. This operation creates an eyelet hole in the knitting and inc 1 st.

k2tog (knit 2 together): Dec 1 st by knitting 2 sts tog.

M1 (make 1): Inc 1 st by picking up the bar between the next st and the st just knit and knitting into it.

Sl marker or sl st(s) (slip marker or slip stitch[es]): Slip a st or sts purlwise from the left needle to the right needle. When slipping a marker, knit the sts before and after it as usual.

YOKE

With color A and longer circular needle, CO enough sts to fit loosely around the neck. The sample starts with 58 sts. Do not join. Knit 2 rows.

BODY

Raglan Shaping

SET-UP ROW (WS): Knit $\frac{1}{3}$ of sts, pm for front sts; knit half of the next $\frac{1}{3}$ of sts, pm for left sleeve; knit $\frac{1}{3}$ of sts, pm for back; knit rem sleeve sts, place unique marker for beg of rnd.

Now you'll work the raglan increases. At the same time, you'll knit eyelets into each front edge, to run the lacing through later.

ROW 1 (RS): K2, yo, k2tog, *knit to 1 st before marker, M1, k1, sl marker, M1; rep from * 3 times more, knit to last 4 sts, k2tog, yo, k2—8 sts inc.

ROWS 2, 4 AND 6 (WS): K4, purl to last 4 sts, k4.

ROWS 3 AND 5: *Knit to 1 st before marker, M1, k1, sl marker, M1; rep from * 3 times more, knit to end.

Rep Rows 1–6 until the raglan length (the diagonal line formed by the raglan increases) reaches the desired measurement less 1" (3cm). End with an RS row.

Join for working in the rnd.

On the next rnd, work some inc across the back section. Count the number of sts in your front and back sections put tog. Find the nearest multiple of 7. Inc as many sts, evenly spaced across the back section, as you need to achieve that number.

Work even in St st for 1" (3cm).

We are starting with the neck here. You are casting on a small amount of stitches as you are creating an open, plunging V-neck and will rapidly increase as you form your raglan sleeves.

We will not be joining, even though we are in fact knitting on circular needles.

Raglan sweaters follow the rule of thirds: $\frac{1}{3}$ of your stitches are devoted to the front part of the sweater; $\frac{1}{3}$ of your stitches are devoted to the back of the sweater; $\frac{1}{3}$ of your stitches are for the sleeves, and you divide that number by 2. You'll place your stitch markers using this rule.

For a CO of 58 sts, it looks like this: K10 (Right Front), pm, k9 (Right Sleeve), pm, k20 (Back), pm, k9 (Left Sleeve), pm, k10 (Left Front).

On Row 1, you knit an eyelet at each end of the row, and you work your raglan increases.

On Rows 3 and 5, you work raglan increases only.

To get the raglan length, measure the length from the child's neck to the underarm with a measuring tape. This should be quite a loose, comfortable measurement, not a tight one.

Why a multiple of 7 stitches? The bottom of the sweater is worked in a k6, p1 rib, so you'll need a multiple of 7 stitches to work the pattern evenly.

Separate Sleeves and Body

NEXT RND: Knit across the front sts to the marker. Remove the marker and place all of the left sleeve sts on a holder. Remove the next marker. Knit across the back sts to the third marker, remove it and place the right sleeve sts on another holder. Leave the beg-of-rnd marker in place.

You should have the front and back sts united on the needle, with a marker at the right underarm. This is the beg of the rnd from now on.

Change to color B and work in garter st for 4 rnds.

Change to color C and begin rib.

NEXT RND: *K6, p1; rep from * to end.

Rep this rnd until sweater reaches desired length less 1" (3cm) for border.

Work in garter st for 6 rnds.

Bind off loosely.

SLEEVES

Put the held sleeve sts on the smaller circular needle. Count your sts. If you have an odd number, dec 1 by k2tog at the beg of the cuff.

Join color B and pm for beg of rnd.

Cuff

RND 1: *K1, p1; rep from * to end.

RND 2: *P1, k1; rep from * to end.

Rep Rnds 1–2 3 times more.

Bind off loosely in patt.

FINISHING

Cord

Pick up your trusty crochet hook and chain for approx 20" (51cm) worth of cord.

Weave in ends. Lace cord through eyelets.

How do you work garter stitch in the round? Knit one round, purl one round; repeat.

We keep the sleeves short and sweet for our kids. They can wear T-shirts under this sweater.

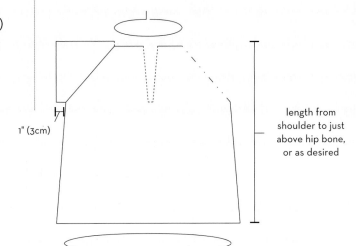

loose neck measurement

1" (3cm)

length from shoulder to just above hip bone, or as desired

chest measurement + 4-6" (10-15cm)

Loba

This design was created by Loba Van Heaugten, a talented Knitchick from Copenhagen. She has a great eye for patterns and knows how to create a comfy fit. This pattern loves you and your curves—notice how the rib resembles an hourglass. Wear this top with long sleeves underneath, or wear it as a tunic!

Pauline

FINISHED MEASUREMENTS

Bust (unstretched): 22 (26½, 31, 35½, 40)" (56 [67, 79, 90, 102]cm)

Length (unstretched): 23¼ (23¾, 24½, 25, 25½)" (59 [60, 62, 64, 65]cm)

FIT

Very close (4" [10cm] or more of negative ease)

YARN

6 (6, 7, 7, 7) skeins Debbie Bliss Cathay (50% cotton, 35% viscose, 15% silk), 109yds [100m] per 50g skein)

    color 25

1 (1, 2, 2, 2) skeins Debbie Bliss Cathay (50% cotton, 35% viscose, 15% silk), 109yds [100m] per 50g skein)

    color 13

NEEDLES

16" and 32" (40cm and 80cm) size US 8 (5mm) circular needles

NOTIONS

stitch markers
2 removable markers
tapestry needle

GAUGE

27 sts and 23 rows = 4" (10cm) in k1, p1 rib, unstretched

NOTES

S2KP (slip 2 together, knit 1, pass slipped stitches over): Slip 2 sts as if to knit them, knit 1 stitch, pass the 2 slipped stitches over the k1 and off the needle (sl2tog, k1, p2sso). This action decreases 2 stitches and creates a vertical decrease.

Make 1: M1R or M1L as needed to create wave pattern.

K2tog (knit 2 together): Dec 1 st by knitting 2 sts tog.

pm (place marker): Slip a premade marker or a loosely knotted piece of scrap yarn in a contrasting color onto the right needle after the stitch just knit to mark a spot in the knitting to refer to on future rows. When you come to a marker, simply slip it from the left-hand needle to the right-hand needle.

SSK (slip, slip, knit): Dec 1 st by slipping 2 sts knitwise 1 at a time, inserting the tip of the left needle into both sts and knitting the 2 sts tog.

p2tog (purl 2 together): Dec 1 st by purling 2 sts tog.

KFB: Inc 1 st by knitting into the next st, and without sliding the st off the left-hand needle, knitting into the back of the same st. Slide old st off left-hand needle, creating 2 new sts on right-hand needle.

BODY

With larger circular needle and MC, CO 150 (180, 210, 240, 270) sts, pm and join for working in the rnd.

Work Rnds 1–44 of Waves Chart twice.

NEXT RND: *P1, k1; rep from * to end.

Rep last rnd 13 times more.

Armhole Shaping

NEXT RND: *Work in est rib patt until there are 61 (76, 91, 100, 111) sts on right-hand needle, BO 14 (14, 14, 20, 24) sts; rep from * once more.

CAP SLEEVES

NEXT RND (RS): Work in est rib patt across first side, use backward-loop method (see page 19) to CO 30 (32, 36, 42, 48) sts, work in rib across second side, CO 30 (32, 36, 42, 48) sts—182 (216, 254, 284, 318) sts.

Pm and join for working in the rnd.

Work in est rib patt for 16 (14, 10, 8, 6) rnds.

Change to CC.

NEXT RND: Rib 77 (91, 109, 121, 135), place removable marker in next st, rib 91 (109, 127, 141, 159), place removable marker in next st, rib to end of rnd.

Shoulder Shaping

Dec on every rnd as foll: *Rib to 1 st before marked st, remove marker, S2KP, replace marker in st just made; rep from * once more, rib to end of rnd—4 sts dec.

Dec as set until 120 (128, 132, 148, 162) sts rem, changing to shorter needle when necessary. AT THE SAME TIME, after 5 rnds have been worked in CC, change to MC for 9 rnds, then change to CC for remainder of top.

NEXT RND: *K2tog; rep from * to end—60 (64, 66, 74, 81) sts.

Knit 1 rnd. BO.

FINISHING

Weave in ends. Do not block.

18 (19½, 20, 22½, 24½)"
(46 [50, 51, 57, 62]cm)

23¼ (23¾, 24¼, 25, 25½)"
(59 [60, 62, 64, 65]cm)

22 (26½, 31, 35½, 40)"
(56 [67, 79, 90, 102]cm)

Waves Chart

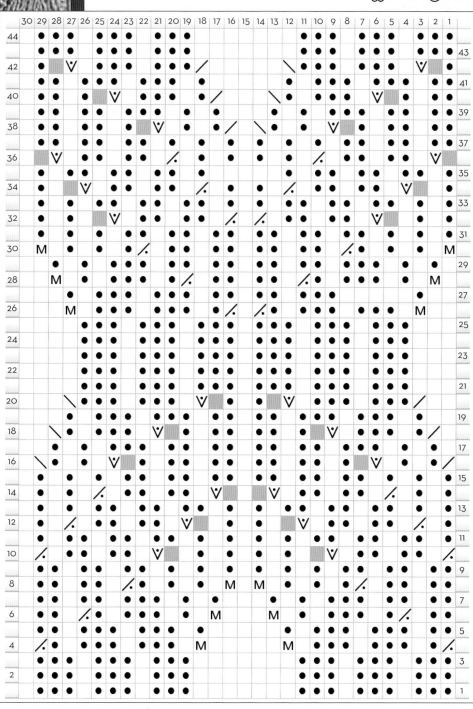

Legend

☐	Knit	Ⅴ	kfb
●	Purl	▨	no stitch
⁄.	p2tog	⁄	k2tog
M	make 1	＼	ssk

Pam

At some point, I became a corporate sassafrass and realized, man, I need something lively to wear to the office. I designed *Pam* (yes, I'm a diehard fan of *The Office*) thinking of that young woman behind the reception desk, although this top is equally fitting for the power player in the board room. It's a top with some attitude, and yet not teetering on hoochie.

Marcelle

FINISHED MEASUREMENTS

Measure your bust and add 2–3" (5–8cm) for ease.
Sample measurements:
Bust: 36" (91cm)
Length: 24" (61cm)

FIT

Standard

YARN

7 skeins Karabella Yarns Zodiac (100% cotton, 98yds [90m] per 50g skein)
color 411 Golden Mustard (MC)

2 skeins Karabella Yarns Zodiac
color 415 Black (CC)

NEEDLES

32" (80cm) size US 7 (4.5mm) circular needle

NOTIONS

long stitch markers
removable marker
tapestry needle
crochet hook

GAUGE

19 sts and 25 rows = 4" (10 cm) in St st

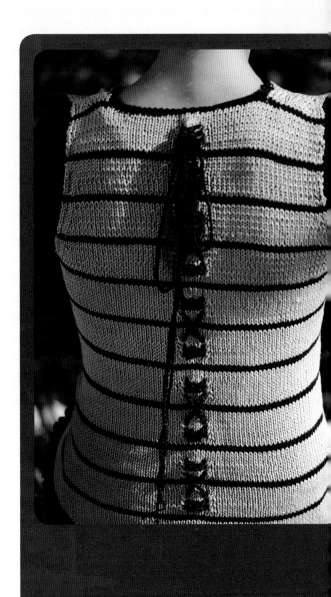

NOTES

pm (place marker): Slip a premade marker or a loosely knotted piece of scrap yarn in a contrasting color onto the right needle after the stitch just knit to mark a spot in the knitting to refer to on future rows. When you come to a marker, simply slip it from the left-hand needle to the right-hand needle.

k2tog (knit 2 together): Dec 1 st by knitting 2 sts tog.

yo (yarn over): Wrap the working yarn around the needle, and knit the next st as usual. This operation creates an eyelet hole in the knitting and inc 1 st.

SSK (slip, slip, knit): Dec 1 st by slipping 2 sts knitwise 1 at a time, inserting the tip of the left needle into both sts and knitting the 2 sts tog.

Sl marker or sl st(s) (slip marker or slip stitch[es]): Slip a st or sts purlwise from the left needle to the right needle. When slipping a marker, knit the sts before and after it as usual.

STRIPE PATTERN

RNDS 1, 2, 4, 6 AND 8–11: Knit with MC.

RNDS 3, 5 AND 7: Knit with MC; on back panel k to 4 sts before center back marker, k2tog, yo, k2, sm, k1, yo, ssk.

RNDS 12–13: Knit with CC.

Rep Rnds 1–13 for stripe patt.

PICOT HEM

We are beginning with a picot hem.

With CC, CO the number of sts required for your bust size plus 8–9" (20–23cm) for ease. Join for working in the rnd. Pm at beg of rnd.

Knit 3 rnds.

EYELET RND: *K2tog, yo; rep from * to end.

Knit 2 rnds.

Fold your hem inward along the yarn-over perforation, toward the Wrong Side.

Pick up 1 st from the outside of the cast-on edge and k2tog—your second st is already on your left-hand needle—and you're golden.

If it sounds out of body to you, think of it this way: You are stacking stitches. You are stacking the stitch already there with the stitch above it, and knitting the two together.

K2tog around, securing the picot hem.

BODY

Knit 1 more rnd with CC, then change to MC and beg Stripe Pattern. Knit 2 rnds.

SET-UP RND: Knit, placing a second marker at the halfway point of the rnd (i.e., after 99 sts, if your CO was 198) and a 3rd marker halfway between the previous two markers on the back panel for lacing eyelets.

The second marker will show you where to place the shaping decreases.
The third marker will show you where to place the lacing eyelets

Oh, and by the way—AT THE SAME TIME, when body measures about half desired length to armhole, dec for waist on every 4th rnd 7 times as foll: *SSK, knit to 2 sts before marker, k2tog, sl marker, SSK, knit to last 2 sts, k2tog—4 sts dec.

Work even until top measures desired length to armhole (approx 15" [38cm]).

Armhole depth: Measure straight down from the top of your shoulder to the top of your bra.

FRONT

Armhole Shaping

BO 8 sts, knit to 8 sts before second side marker, BO 16 sts, knit to last 8 sts, BO 8 sts. Cut yarn. Join yarn to front sts with RS facing.

Row 1 (RS): K1, k2tog, knit to last 3 sts, SSK, k1—2 sts dec.

Row 2 (WS): Purl.

Rep these 2 rows until the number of sts rem equals your desired cross-back measurement.

Neck Shaping

Now it's time to think about the V-neck. First, you need to decide how deep you want it to be, and figure out where that falls in relation to the depth of the armholes. On the top shown, the V-neck is 5½" (14cm) deep and the armholes are 8½" (22cm) deep. That means after the armhole shaping was finished, we knit even until the armholes measured 3" (8cm)—in other words, 8½"–5½" = 3"—before beginning the neck shaping. If you don't want to do math here, just begin the neck shaping as soon as you've finished the armhole shaping, and it will work out fine! Larger sizes (anything over bust 40" [102cm]) should start the neck decreases right away in any case, as they have to decrease away more sts in a relatively shorter space. Find the center st of the front and place a removable marker in it.

Row 1 (RS): Knit to marked st, BO marked st, knit to end.

Right Shoulder

Next Row (WS): Purl.

Next Row (RS): K1, SSK, knit to end—1 st dec.

Rep these 2 rows until shoulder reaches desired width or you reach the desired armhole depth, whichever comes first. Work even, if necessary, to desired armhole depth. BO.

Left shoulder

Join yarn with WS facing.

Next Row (WS): Purl.

Next Row (RS): Knit to last 3 sts, k2tog, k1—1 st dec.

Rep these 2 rows until shoulder reaches desired width or you reach the desired armhole depth, whichever comes first. (Make sure you have the same number of sts as for the right shoulder as the left shoulder!) Work even, if necessary, to desired armhole depth. BO.

BACK

Join yarn to back sts with RS facing. Work the armhole shaping exactly as for the front, then work even until armholes measure same as front to shoulder. BO.

FINISHING

Use mattress stitch (see page 32) to seam the shoulders. With CC, work a round of single crochet around the armholes and neck. Weave in ends.

With CC, crochet a chain 120" (305cm) long. Lace through back eyelets.

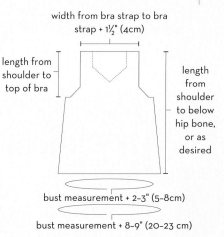

width from bra strap to bra strap + 1½" (4cm)

length from shoulder to top of bra

length from shoulder to below hip bone, or as desired

bust measurement + 2–3" (5–8cm)

bust measurement + 8–9" (20–23 cm)

The shoulder strap width should be somewhere in the neighborhood of 2"–3½" (5–9cm). Remember that you're going to add crochet edgings on either side later, so don't make the strap too wide to start with.

Same as front to shoulder = The armholes on the back are the same length as the armholes on the front.

Raven

Through my work directing Breast Cancer Public Service Announcements, and during my time at *BUST*, I've met many brave women over the years who are true survivors. When we first started thinking about this book, I knew instantly I wanted to create a pattern to pay homage to all the women I've met over the course of my career. This sexy lace top with hot pink piping seemed like the way to go.

Marcelle

FINISHED MEASUREMENTS
Bust: 33 (35, 37, 39, 41, 43)" (84 [89, 94, 99, 104, 109]cm)
Length: 21 (21, 22, 23, 24, 24)" (54 [54, 56, 59, 61, 61]cm)

FIT
Close

YARN
3 (3, 4, 4, 5, 5) skeins Lorna's Laces Shepherd Sport Solid (100% superwash wool; 200 yds [183m] per 70g skein)
color Black (MC)

1 (1, 1, 1, 2, 2) skein(s) Debbie Bliss Pure Cashmere (100% cashmere, 49 yds [45m] per 25g skein)
color #07 Hot Pink (CC)

NEEDLES
16" and 32" (40cm and 80cm) size US 8 (5mm) circular needles

NOTIONS
stitch holders
tapestry needle
crochet hook

GAUGE
16 sts and 24 rows = 4" (10cm) in St st

NOTES

pm (place marker): Slip a premade marker or a loosely knotted piece of scrap yarn in a contrasting color onto the right needle after the stitch just knit to mark a spot in the knitting to refer to on future rows. When you come to a marker, simply slip it from the left-hand needle to the right-hand needle.

sm or sl st(s) (slip marker or slip stitch[es]): Slip a st or sts purlwise from the left needle to the right needle. When slipping a marker, knit the sts before and after it as usual.

k2tog or k3tog (knit 2 or 3 together): Dec 1 st by knitting 2 sts tog or dec 2 sts by knitting 3 sts tog.

yo (yarn over): Wrap the working yarn around the needle, and knit the next st as usual. This operation creates an eyelet hole in the knitting and inc 1 st.

M1 (make 1): Inc 1 st by picking up the bar between the next st and the st just knit and knitting into it.

SSK (slip, slip, knit): Dec 1 st by slipping 2 sts knitwise 1 at a time, inserting the tip of the left needle into both sts and knitting the 2 sts tog.

psso (pass slipped stitch over): When instructed to knit 1, slip 1, the pattern may then tell you to pass the slipped st over the st just knit, dec 1 st. Simply follow the pattern as written, passing the slipped st over any previous st(s) as indicated.

UPPER BACK

With MC, CO 58 (60, 62, 64, 66, 68) sts.

Lace Inset

ROWS 1–4: Work in St st, beg with a knit row.

ROW 5 (RS): K11 (12, 13, 14, 15, 16), pm, *k2tog, yo; rep from * to last 11 (12, 13, 14, 15, 16) sts, pm, knit to end.

ROWS 6–8 AND ALL ROWS NOT OTHERWISE SPECIFIED: Work in St st.

ROW 9 (RS): Knit to marker, sm, *k2tog, yo; rep from * to marker, knit to end.

ROW 13 (RS): Knit to marker, sm, k2, *k2tog, yo; rep from * to 2 sts before marker, knit to end.

ROW 17 (RS): Knit to marker, sm, k4, *k2tog, yo; rep from * to 4 sts before marker, knit to end.

ROW 21 (RS): Knit to marker, sm, k6, *k2tog, yo; rep from * to 6 sts before marker, knit to end.

ROW 25 (RS): Knit to marker, sm, k8, *k2tog, yo; rep from * to 8 sts before marker, knit to end.

ROW 29 (RS): Knit to marker, sm, k10, *k2tog, yo; rep from * to 10 sts before marker, knit to end.

ROW 33 (RS): Knit to marker, sm, k12, *k2tog, yo; rep from * 3 times more, knit to end.

ROW 37 (RS): Knit to marker, sm, k15, *k2tog, yo; rep from * twice more, knit to end.

ROW 39 (RS): K1, M1, knit to last st, M1, k1—2 sts inc.

ROW 41 (RS): K1, M1, knit to marker, sm, k16, *k2tog, yo; rep from * once more, knit to last st, M1, k1—2 sts inc.

ROW 43 (RS): K1, M1, knit to last st, M1, k1—2 sts inc.

ROW 45 (RS): K1, M1, knit to marker, sm, k18, k2tog, yo, knit to last st, M1, k1—2 sts inc.

ROW 46 (WS): Purl.

For size 33 only, stop here—66 sts.

Sizes 35 (37, 39, 41, 43):

NEXT ROW (RS): K1, M1, knit to last st, M1, k1—2 sts inc.

Purl 1 WS row.

Rep last 2 rows 0 (1, 2, 3, 4) times more—70 (74, 78, 82, 86) sts.

All sizes: Place sts on holder or spare needle.

UPPER FRONT

The upper front is worked in 2 parts until joining at the base of the V-neck.

Left Side

With MC, CO 12 (12, 14, 14, 16, 16) sts.

Work even in St st for 1½ (1¾, 2¼, 2½, 3, 3)" (4 [5, 6, 7, 8, 8]cm), ending with a WS row.

INC ROW (RS): K1, M1, knit to end—1 st inc.

Purl 1 WS row.

Rep last 2 rows 13 (13, 11, 11, 9, 9) times more—26 (26, 26, 26, 26, 26) sts.

INC ROW (RS): K1, M1, knit to last st, M1, k1—2 sts inc.

Purl 1 WS row.

Rep last 2 rows 2 (3, 4, 5, 6, 7) times more—32 (34, 36, 38, 40, 42) sts. Place sts on holder or spare needle.

Right Side

With MC and longer circular needle, CO 12 (12, 14, 14, 16, 16) sts.

Work even in St st for 1½ (1¾, 2¼, 2½, 3, 3)" (4 [5, 6, 7, 8, 8]cm), ending with a WS row.

INC ROW (RS): Knit to last st, M1, k1—1 st inc.

Purl 1 WS row.

Rep last 2 rows 13 (13, 11, 11, 9, 9) times more—26 (26, 26, 26, 26, 26) sts.

INC ROW (RS): K1, M1, knit to last st, M1, k1—2 sts inc.

Purl 1 WS row.

Rep last 2 rows 2 (3, 4, 5, 6, 7) times more—32 (34, 36, 38, 40, 42) sts. Leave sts on needle.

Join Left and Right Sides

NEXT ROW (RS): Beg at right side, k1, M1, knit across rem right side sts, then knit across left side sts to last st, M1, k1—66 (70, 74, 78, 82, 86) sts.

Purl 1 WS row.

Join Upper Back and Upper Front

Knit across front sts, pm, knit across back sts, pm, join for working in the rnd—132 (140, 148, 156, 164, 172) sts.

Lower Body

Knit 1 rnd even.

NEXT RND: K1, yo, SSK, knit to 3 sts before marker, k2tog, yo, k1, sm, k1, yo, SSK, knit to last 3 sts, k2tog, yo, k1.

Rep these 2 rnds until top measures 20 (20, 21, 22, 23, 23)" (51 [51, 54, 56, 59, 59]cm) from shoulders.

Hem

EYELET RND: *K2, yo, k2tog; rep from * to end.

Knit 1 rnd. Purl 1 rnd. Knit 1 rnd. Purl 1 rnd. BO.

SLEEVES (MAKE 2 ALIKE)

Seam shoulders. With shorter circular needle and MC, beg at underarm with RS facing, pick up and k70 (70, 74, 74, 78, 78) sts around armhole. Pm for beg of rnd.

RND 1 AND ODD RNDS THROUGH RND 15: Knit.

RND 2: K2, *k2tog, yo, k2; rep from * to end.

RND 4: K1, *k2tog, yo, k2; rep from * to last st, k1.

RND 6: K2, *yo, k2tog, k2tog; rep from * to last 4 sts, yo, k2tog, k2—54 (54, 57, 57, 60, 60) sts.

RND 8: K2, *yo, k2tog, k1; rep from * to last st, k1.

RND 10: K2, *yo, k3tog; rep from * to last 4 (4, 3, 3, 2, 2) sts, yo, k2tog, k2 (2, 1, 1, 0, 0)—42 (42, 44, 44, 46, 46) sts.

RND 12: K2, *yo, k2tog; rep from * to last 2 sts, k2.

RND 14: K2, *yo, sl1, k1, psso; rep from * to last 2 sts, k2.

Rep Rnds 12–15 until sleeve measures 5½ (5½, 5½, 6, 6, 6)" (14 [14, 14, 15, 15, 15]cm) from armhole.

Knit 5 rnds.

NEXT RND: Knit, dec 10 (10, 12, 8, 10, 10) sts evenly spaced around—32 (32, 32, 36, 36, 36) sts.

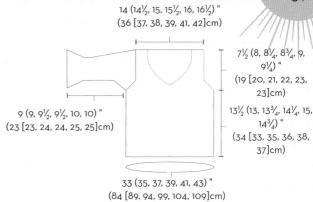

14 (14½, 15, 15½, 16, 16½) "
(36 [37, 38, 39, 41, 42]cm)

7½ (8, 8¼, 8¾, 9, 9¼) "
(19 [20, 21, 22, 23, 23]cm)

13½ (13, 13¾, 14¼, 15, 14¾) "
(34 [33, 35, 36, 38, 37]cm)

9 (9, 9½, 9½, 10, 10) "
(23 [23, 24, 24, 25, 25]cm)

33 (35, 37, 39, 41, 43) "
(84 [89, 94, 99, 104, 109]cm)

CUFF

RNDS 1–2: *K3, p1; rep from * to end.

RND 3: *K1, M1, k2, p1; rep from * to end—40 (40, 40, 45, 45, 45) sts.

RNDS 4–5: *K4, p1; rep from * to end.

RND 6: *K3, M1, k1, p1; rep from * to end—48 (48, 48, 54, 54, 54) sts.

RNDS 7–8: *K5, p1; rep from * to end.

RND 9: *K1, M1, k4, p1; rep from * to end—56 (56, 56, 63, 63, 63) sts.

RNDS 10–11: *K6, p1; rep from * to end.

RND 12: *K5, M1, k1, p1; rep from * to end—64 (64, 64, 72, 72, 72) sts.

RNDS 13–14: *K7, p1; rep from * to end.

RND 15: *K1, M1, k6, p1; rep from * to end—72 (72, 72, 81, 81, 81) sts.

RNDS 16–17: *K8, p1; rep from * to end.

RND 18: *K7, M1, k1, p1; rep from * to end—80 (80, 80, 90, 90, 90) sts.

RNDS 19–20: *K9, p1; rep from * to end.

RND 21: *K1, M1, k8, p1; rep from * to end—88 (88, 88, 99, 99, 99) sts.

RNDS 22–23: *K10, p1; rep from * to end.

RND 24: *K9, M1, k1, p1; rep from * to end—96 (96, 96, 108, 108, 108) sts.

RNDS 25–27: *K11, p1; rep from * to end.

HEM

Knit 1 rnd. Purl 1 rnd. Knit 1 rnd. Purl 1 rnd. BO.

FINISHING

With CC, work 1 single crochet in each st around cuffs and bottom of body. With MC, work 1 single crochet in each st around front neckline.

Weave in ends.

Thelma & Louise

The *Thelma & Louise Wrap* is the perfect project for a long road trip. It's a basic pattern with lots of straight knitting, so you can turn your attention to other things—the view, games, conversation—and not have to concentrate too hard. I knitted most of this piece on a journey between Copenhagen and Oslo, a relatively short drive but with lots of stops. The simple pattern made it easy to put down and pick up again.

As the piece grows, you have an instant blanket! If you're substituting yarn, keep in mind that the final piece is quite large, so choose a lighter-weight yarn. The Manos silk blend is a great combination of chunky and soft, yet light.

Pauline

FINISHED MEASUREMENTS
One size fits most.
The wrap shown will comfortably fit up to a 44" (112cm) bust.
See schematic for finished measurements.

YARN
9 skeins Manos del Uruguay Silk Blend Semi-Solid (70% extrafine wool, 30% silk, 150 yds [135m] per 50g skein)
color #300U Rust

NEEDLES
32" (80cm) size US 6 (4mm) circular needle
16" and 32" (40cm and 80cm) size US 7 (4.5mm) circular needles
32" (80cm) size US 8 (5mm) circular needle

NOTIONS
tapestry needle
sewing machine for steeking
sewing thread in contrasting color
sewing needle
kilt pin for fastening

GAUGE
21 sts and 32 rows = 4" (10cm) in St st with size US 6 (4mm) needles
20 sts and 29 rows = 4" (10cm) in St st with size US 7 (4.5mm) needles
19 sts and 27 rows = 4" (10cm) in St st with size US 8 (5mm) needles

NOTES
S2KP (slip 2 together, knit 1, pass slipped stitches over): Slip 2 sts as if to knit them, knit 1 stitch, pass the 2 slipped stitches over the k1 and off the needle (sl2tog, k1, p2sso). This action decreases 2 stitches and creates a vertical decrease.

p2tog (purl 2 together): Dec 1 st by purling 2 sts tog.

yo (yarn over): Wrap the working yarn around the needle clockwise, and work the next st as usual. This operation creates an eyelet hole in the knitting and inc 1 st.

BOTTOM BORDER

With US 8 (5mm) needle, CO 285 sts.

ROWS 1–3: Knit.

ROW 4 (WS): *P2tog, yo; rep from * to last st, p1.

ROWS 5–7: Knit.

ROW 8: Purl.

Rep Rows 1–8 twice more—24 rows worked.

BODY

ROW 1 (RS): Knit all sts.

ROW 2 (WS): K7, purl to last 7 sts, k7.

ROW 3: Knit all sts.

ROW 4: (P2tog, yo) 3 times, p2tog, purl to last 8 sts, (p2tog, yo) 3 times, p2tog—2 sts dec'd.

ROW 5: Knit all sts.

ROW 6: K7, purl to last 7 sts, k7.

ROW 7: Knit all sts.

ROW 8: Purl all sts.

Rep Rows 1–8 until piece measures 16" (40cm).

Change to US 7 (4.5mm) needle and cont in est patt until piece measures 27" (70cm).

Change to US 6 (4mm) needle and cont in est patt until piece measures 31" (80cm).

TOP BORDER

Work in garter st (knit every row) for 1" (3cm).

Bind off.

FINISHING

Steeking

Now we measure out the armholes to be steeked. (For steeking instructions with photos, see pages 106–107.)

Fold the piece in half lengthwise to find center back.

From center back, measure 10" (25cm) to left and right to place the armholes. Measure 6" (16cm) down from the top edge to mark the top of each armhole. Measure 9" (23cm) down from the top of each armhole to mark armhole depth. The armhole will be 3 sts wide.

Use contrasting thread and a hand-basting stitch to mark each armhole. Run your basting line right up the middle st column to keep it straight.

Machine-sew twice around each armhole.

Take a sharp pair of scissors and cut along the hand-basted line. Don't cut through the machine stitching.

To work armhole edging, pick up and knit 86 sts around armhole with shorter US 7 (4.5mm) circular needle. Knit 7 rnds. BO.

Weave in ends. Steam block lightly, if desired.

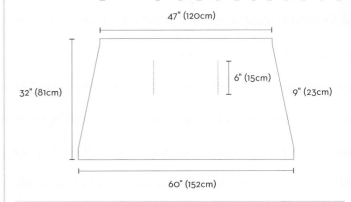

Knitting Blind

Can you knit without looking? It's a handy skill to have, especially if you're knitting in front of the television (where you can usually find the Knitchicks working on their projects). This is a great project for learning this skill. Get a feel for the stitches and how they move along the needle. Start out with knitting one stitch while looking away, then slowly build up the numbers. Check your knitting regularly to see how you're doing.

47" (120cm)

6" (15cm)

32" (81cm)

9" (23cm)

60" (152cm)

Measure, measure and measure again! You get only one chance to cut.

Summer

Knitwear is not just for winter! Lightweight, flowing and made from a cool mercerized cotton, the *Summer* top is great for a hot day in the city. Play around with bright colors for daytime wear and more subdued shades for evening. This top looks great anytime, day or night!

Pauline

FINISHED MEASUREMENTS

32"–38" (40–46, 48+)" (81–97 [102–117, 122+]cm)
Measure your bust and add 1"–2" (3–5cm) for ease.
Sample measurements:
Bust: 35" (89cm)
Length from shoulder: 20" (51cm)

Note: See the pattern for instructions on customizing the sweater to fit your measurements and desired fit.

FIT
Close

YARN

3 skeins Isager Bomuld (100% mercerized cotton; 229yds [209m] per 50g skein)
   color 004 light spring green (MC)
1 skein Isager Bomuld (100% mercerized cotton; 229yds [209m] per 50g skein)
   color 49 purple (CC)

NEEDLES
24" (60cm) size US 3 (3.25mm) circular needle

NOTIONS
2 regular stitch markers
4 removable stitch markers or safety pins
stitch holder
tapestry needle

GAUGE
28 sts and 37 rows = 4" (10cm) in St st
23 sts and 46 rows = 4" (10cm) in garter st

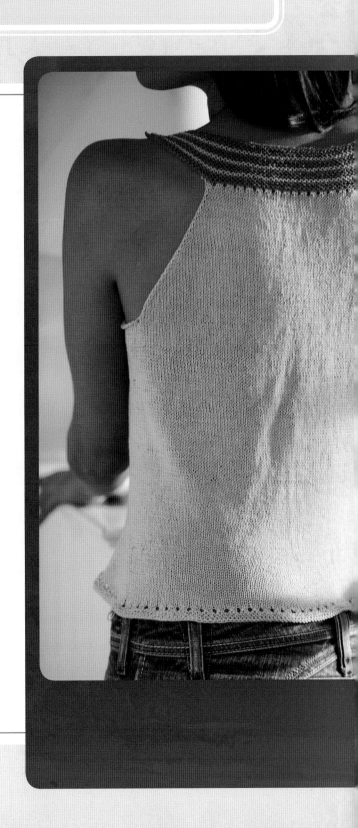

NOTES

pm (place marker): Slip a premade marker or a loosely knotted piece of scrap yarn in a contrasting color onto the right needle after the stitch just knit to mark a spot in the knitting to refer to on future rows. When you come to a marker, simply slip it from the left-hand needle to the right-hand needle.

M1 (make 1): Inc 1 st by picking up the bar between the next st and the st just knit and knitting into it.

Sl marker or sl st(s) (slip marker or slip stitch[es]): Slip a st or sts purlwise from the left needle to the right needle. When slipping a marker, knit the sts before and after it as usual.

yo (yarn over): Wrap the working yarn around the needle, and work the next st as usual. This operation creates an eyelet hole in the knitting and inc 1 st.

k2tog (knit 2 together): Dec 1 st by knitting 2 sts tog.

STRIPE PATTERN FOR YOKE

RND 1: Knit with CC.

RND 2: Purl with CC.

RND 3: Knit with CC.

RND 4: Purl with CC.

RND 5: Knit with MC.

RND 6: Purl with MC.

Rep Rnds 1–6 for stripe patt.

YOKE

CO approx 116 (128, 140) sts.

Join for working in the rnd. Pm at beg of rnd, and place a second marker at halfway point of rnd (after 58 [64, 70] sts).

Working in stripe patt, inc on 1st rnd, then every other rnd as foll: *K1, M1, knit to 1 st before marker, M1, k1, sl marker; rep from * once more—4 sts inc.

Cont as set until approx 20 (20, 26) rnds total have been worked.

Count the number of sts on the needle. Subtract 68 from this number, then divide the result by 2. Use removable markers to mark off this number of sts in the center of each half of yoke. For example, if you have 156 sts total, pm on either side of the center 44 sts, back and front. Note: Larger sizes (approx 44" [112cm] and up) may wish to use more than 68 sts in this calculation if subtracting 68 results in too wide front/back sections. In that case, subtracting 72–80 sts should give a better fit.

BO all sts loosely.

The nature of cotton and the gauge of this yarn make hiding yarn joins difficult. Regardless of how much yarn you have left, always ensure you join the new yarn in at the underarm.

This top is knit from the top down, starting with the fitted neck band. The neck band is knit in garter stitch, which is accomplished by alternating rows of knit and purl when working in the round. These st counts are adjustable, but it helps if you choose a number divisible by 4.

You can make the yoke deeper or shallower according to your preference, but it will look best if you end with Rnd 2 of the stripe pattern.

Yep, you read that correctly. Bind off all stitches. For the next part of the top, the stitches will be picked up from the bound-off edge.

UPPER BACK/FRONT (WORKED ALIKE)

With MC, RS of yoke facing, pick up and knit 1 st in each st between the markers (in our example, 44 sts).

Row 1 (WS): Sl 1, *p2, yo; rep from * to last 2 or 3 sts, purl to end.

Note: Row 1 creates a line of eyelets and also adds a bit of fullness to the top.

Row 2 (RS): Sl 1, knit to end.

Row 3: Sl 1, purl to end.

You will now inc 1 st at each end of every RS row, as foll:

Row 4 (RS): Sl 1, k1, M1, knit to last 2 sts, M1, k2.

Row 5: Sl 1, purl to end.

Rep Rows 4–5 until the number of sts on the needle is equal to half the total sts needed for your bust size, less 15 sts for underarms.

Note: On the last WS row, do not slip the first st; purl it normally instead.

Place sts on holder while you work the second piece. When the second piece is finished, leave it on the needle.

Lower Body

Here the 2 sides are joined.

Knit across all sts on needle, use cable cast-on method (see page 23) to CO 15 sts for underarm, knit all sts from holder, CO 15 sts for underarm. Pm and join for working in the rnd.

Note: You can also use the backward-loop cast on (see page 19) at the underarms, but the cable method gives a neater edge.

Now you can knit to your heart's content. Or at least for as long as you want the garment to be. Top shown measures 11½" (29cm) from underarm to top of border.

BORDER

Next Rnd: *K1, k2tog, yo; rep from * around.

Work next 6 rows in garter st (knit and purl alternate rnds).

BO loosely.

FINISHING

Weave in ends, put on the top and wear it in the sun (don't forget your sunscreen)!

Now you will work back and front separately until rejoining at the underarm. This can be in the main color or in stripes like the yoke.

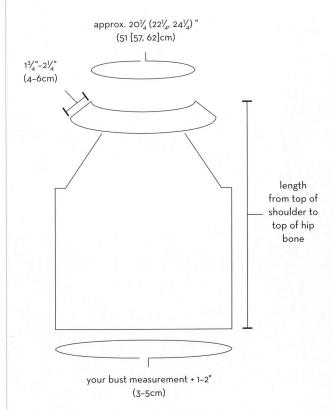

approx. 20¼ (22¼, 24¼)"
(51 [57, 62]cm)

1¾"-2¼"
(4-6cm)

length from top of shoulder to top of hip bone

your bust measurement + 1-2"
(3-5cm)

Moni

This is a bog standard, raglan sleeve, all-in-one jumper. The unique part is that it's totally reversible! OK, that makes it two jumpers...and that's double the fun (but not twice the difficulty). It's really a simple concept: Make two jumpers; turn one inside out and bind off the waist, neck and sleeves to its corresponding partner. Choose yarns of a similar hue but in different colors. To make the most of the dual-tones, use that second color for the neck, sleeves and waist. This and other possibilities are what make Moni so much fun to knit.

Rowan's kidsilk haze is as light as a feather but fiendishly warm. Two layers of this and you'll stay toasty in the most arctic of climes, but without the bulk. You'll be able to wear it under your winter jacket without busting out at the seams, maintaining a chic, slim look.

Don't need it so warm? Make it just once and keep it a single-layer sweater. This is a handy no-nonsense raglan-knit-in-the-round pattern that you can use time and time again.

Pauline

FINISHED MEASUREMENTS

Bust: 35¼ (39¼, 43½, 47½, 50½)" (89 [100, 110, 120, 129]cm)
Length: 24¼ (24¾, 25¼, 25¾, 26¼)" (62 [63, 64, 66, 67]cm)

FIT
Standard

YARN
4 (5, 6, 6, 6) skeins Rowan Kidsilk Haze (70% super kid mohair, 30% silk; 227 yds (207m) per 25g skein) in each of the foll colors:

> color #579 Splendour (MC1)
> color #606 Candy Girl (MC2)

Note: Each layer is made in a different main color (MC1 and MC2). Cuffs and collar are worked using 1 strand of each color held tog.

NEEDLES
16" and 24" (40cm and 60cm) size US 3 (3.25mm) circular needles
size US 3 (3.25mm) DPNs

NOTIONS
stitch markers
stitch holders
tapestry needle
smooth contrasting scrap yarn for provisional cast on

GAUGE
24 sts and 36 rows = 4" (10cm) in St st

NOTES

M1L (make 1 left): Inc 1 st by lifting the bar between the st just knit and the next st onto the left-hand needle and knitting it through the back loop to prevent creating a hole in the knitted fabric.

M1R (make 1 right): Inc 1 st by lifting the bar between the st just knit and the next st, twisting it, and placing it onto the left-hand needle and knitting it to prevent creating a hole in the knitted fabric.

pm (place marker): Slip a premade marker or a loosely knotted piece of scrap yarn in a contrasting color onto the right needle after the stitch just knit to mark a spot in the knitting to refer to on future rows. When you come to a marker, simply slip it from the left-hand needle to the right-hand needle.

Sl marker or sl st(s) (slip marker or slip stitch[es]): Slip a st or sts purlwise from the left needle to the right needle. When slipping a marker, knit the sts before and after it as usual.

SSK (slip, slip, knit): Dec 1 st by slipping 2 sts knitwise 1 at a time, inserting the tip of the left needle into both sts and knitting the 2 sts tog.

k2tog (knit 2 together): Dec 1 st by knitting 2 sts tog.

SLEEVES (MAKE 2)

With DPNs and scrap yarn, use the provisional cast on to CO 50 (52, 56, 58, 62) sts. Cut scrap yarn and join MC. Pm and join for working in the rnd. Work even in 3 x 3 rib for 1½" (4 cm).

INC RND: K1, M1L, knit to last st, M1R, k1—2 sts inc.

Work 6 (6, 6, 5, 5) rnds even.

Rep last 7 (7, 7, 6, 6) rnds 14 (16, 17, 19, 20) times more—80 (86, 92, 98, 104) sts.

Work even until sleeve measures 16½ (16½, 17, 17, 17½)" (42 [42, 43, 43, 45]cm). End last rnd 5 (7, 9, 11, 13) sts before marker. Place next 10 (14, 18, 22, 26) sts on holder for underarm. Place rem 70 (72, 74, 76, 78) sts on scrap yarn or spare circular needle while you work second sleeve. Break yarn, leaving a long tail for finishing underarms.

BODY

With longer circular needle and scrap yarn, CO 212 (236, 260, 284, 304) sts. Cut scrap yarn and join MC. Pm for beg of rnd and join for working in the rnd. On first rnd, place a second marker after 106 (118, 130, 142, 152) sts. Work in St st for 16 (16, 16½, 16½, 16½)", (41 [41, 42, 42, 42]cm). End last rnd 5 (7, 9, 11, 13) sts before beg-of-rnd marker. Place next 10 (14, 18, 22, 26) sts on holder for underarm.

YOKE

Unite body and sleeves as foll: With needle holding body sts, pm for beg of rnd, then knit all sts of first sleeve, ignoring held underarm sts. Pm, knit across body sts to 5 (7, 9, 11, 13) sts before second marker. Place next 10 (14, 18, 22, 26) body sts on holder for underarm. Pm, knit all sts of next sleeve onto body needle, again ignoring underarm sts. Pm, knit across rem body sts to end of rnd—332 (352, 372, 392, 408) sts.

*3 x 3 ribbing is worked over a multiple of 6 stitches. Work 3 x 3 rib as follows: *K3, p3; rep from * to end.*

Is the body long enough? Too long? You decide. Remember that what you do for one color, you must do for the other. Also keep in mind that you will later add a ribbing to the bottom of the piece which will add to its length.

If your circulars have a longer needle section (like my Addi lace), the following rounds might feel a little awkward. That's because it's trying to deal with 70 sts where it used to be 10! Never fear, it can be done — squash as much knitting onto the right needle as possible. After three or four rounds, you won't notice the "sleeve squash" as much.

RNDS 1–4: Knit.

RND 5: K1, SSK, *knit to 3 sts before next marker, k2tog, k1, sl marker, k1, SSK; rep from twice more, knit to last 3 sts, k2tog, k1—8 sts dec.

RND 6: Knit.

Rep Rnds 5–6 29 (31, 33, 35, 37) times more—92 (96, 100, 104, 104) sts rem.

NEXT RND: Knit, dec 2 (0, 4, 2, 2) sts evenly spaced around—90 (96, 96, 102, 102) sts.

Do not cut yarn. Remove markers and leave neck sts on holder or spare circular needle while you work second layer.

Join Two Pieces

Now the two pieces become one! If you have enough needles, have both sets of neck sts on them, as if you were going to work a three needle bind off. Alternately, have 1 neck on scrap yarn and 1 on the shorter circular needle. Turn 1 layer inside out and place inside second piece, with WS tog.

For the collar, knit 1 st from the inside layer and 1 st from the outside layer tog as 1 st using 1 strand of each color yarn. With 1 strand of each color held tog, work 3 x 3 rib around, working the 2 layers of neck sts tog as if they were 1. Cont to work in ribbing for 1½" (4cm), or desired length. BO.

CUFFS

Remove the scrap yarn from each layer's cast on and place sts of each piece on needles and/or scrap yarn. Join 1 strand of each color and knit 1 rnd, treating the 2 layers as 1 and dec 2 (4, 2, 4, 2) sts evenly spaced—48 (48, 54, 54, 60) sts. Work 3 x 3 rib for 2½" (7cm). BO.

BODY RIBBING

Remove the scrap yarn from each layer's cast on and place sts of each piece on needles and/or scrap yarn. Join 1 strand of each color and knit 1 rnd, treating the 2 layers as 1 and dec 2 (2, 2, 2, 4) sts evenly spaced—210 (234, 258, 282, 300) sts. Work in 3 x 3 rib for 1¼" (4cm). BO.

FINISHING

Join underarm seams using Kitchener st (see pages 32–33), joining each layer separately.

Weave in ends.

At some stage, the longer needles will need to be changed for shorter ones. You will "feel" this when there are just enough stitches to go around. Downsize before the work begins to stretch!

This first row will be difficult and will require extra concentration, but it will be smooth sailing on subsequent rows.

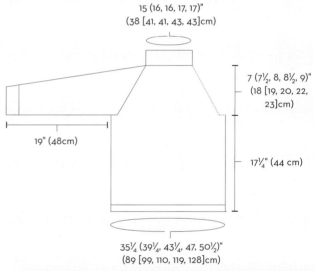

15 (16, 16, 17, 17)"
(38 [41, 41, 43, 43]cm)

7 (7½, 8, 8½, 9)"
(18 [19, 20, 22, 23]cm)

19" (48cm)

17¼" (44 cm)

35¼ (39¼, 43¼, 47, 50½)"
(89 [99, 110, 119, 128]cm)

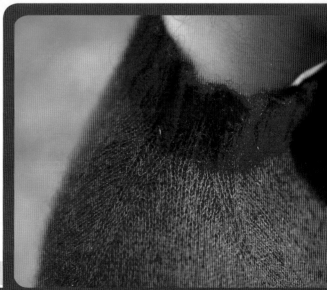

Layla

Autumn in New York City, where I live, is a wonderland for knitters. All the projects we've been sitting on all summer come out of the closet, and this includes the nice wool yarn I buy for a steal during the off-season. This yarn, by Karabella, was the first thing I grabbed when I decided to design an autumnal top that I could wear to work or while running errands as the weather turns crisp. The biggest challenge? To make it feminine (hence the mesh pattern in the sleeves), yet not too snug.

Marcelle

FINISHED MEASUREMENTS

Measure your chest and add 1"–2" (3–5cm) for ease.
Sample size:
Bust: 34" (86cm)
Length: 22½" (57cm)

FIT

Close

YARN

6 skeins Karabella Yarns Aurora 8 Space Dyed (100% extrafine merino wool, 98yds [90m] per 50g skein)
color 7

NEEDLES

16" and 29" (40cm and 74cm) size US 8 (5mm) circular needles
size US 8 (5mm) DPNs (optional)

NOTIONS

stitch markers
stitch holders
tapestry needle
crochet hook

GAUGE

Gauge: 17 sts and 24 rows = 4" (10cm) in St st

NOTES

pm (place marker): Slip a premade marker or a loosely knotted piece of scrap yarn in a contrasting color onto the right needle after the stitch just knit to mark a spot in the knitting to refer to on future rows. When you come to a marker, simply slip it from the right-hand needle to the left-hand needle.

M1 (make 1): Inc 1 st by picking up the bar between the next st and the st just knit and knitting into it.

Sl marker or sl st(s) (slip marker or slip stitch[es]): Slip a st or sts purlwise from the left needle to the right needle. When slipping a marker, knit the sts before and after it as usual.

yo (yarn over): Wrap the working yarn around the needle, and work the next st as usual. This operation creates an eyelet hole in the knitting and inc 1 st.

k2tog (knit 2 together): Dec 1 st by knitting 2 sts tog.

KFB (knit 1 front and back): Inc 1 st by knitting into the next st, and without sliding the st off the left-hand needle, knitting into the back of the same st. Slide old st off left-hand needle, creating 2 new sts on right-hand needle.

YOKE

With shorter circular needle, CO enough sts to fit loosely around your neck. Pm and join for working in the round. The sample starts with 70 sts.

Eyelet Neck Edge

RND 1: Knit 1 rnd.

RND 2: *K2tog, yo; rep from * to end.

Raglan Shaping

SET-UP ROW (WS): Knit ⅓ of sts, pm for front sts; knit half of the next ⅓ of sts, pm for left sleeve; knit ⅓ of sts, pm for back; knit rem sleeve sts, place unique marker for beg of rnd.

Now you'll begin working the raglan increases.

RND 4: *KFB, knit to 1 st before marker, KFB, sl marker, KFB, [k2tog, yo] to 1 st before marker, KFB, sl marker; rep from * once more—8 sts inc.

RND 5: Knit.

Rep Rnds 4–5 until the number of sts in the back and front sections put together equals the number of sts needed for desired bust measurement. Change to longer circular needle when necessary.

BODY

Place the sleeve sts on holders as foll:

NEXT RND: *Knit to marker, sl marker, place all sleeve sts on a holder, remove next marker; rep from * once more.

Now you have all of the body sts together on the needle, with a marker at each underarm.

Your cast on should be an even number of stitches.

These increases give the sweater its A-line shape.

Raglan sweaters follow the rule of thirds: ⅓ of your stitches are devoted to the front part of the sweater; ⅓ of your stitches are devoted to the back of the sweater; ⅓ of your stitches are for the sleeves, and you divide that number by 2. You'll place your stitch markers using this rule.

For a cast on of 70 stitches, it looks like this: K23 for front, pm, k12 for left sleeve, pm, k23 for back, pm, k12 for right sleeve.

Work in St st on the body sts.

On every 10th rnd, work inc as foll: K1, M1, knit to 1 st before marker, M1, k1, sl marker, knit to end—2 sts inc.

When sweater measures approx 21½" (55cm) from shoulder, or desired length minus 1" (3cm), work the bottom edging.

Knit to marker. Turn, leaving rem sts on needle.

NEXT ROW: Sl 1, knit to end.

Rep last row twice more.

EYELET ROW (RS): Sl 1, *k2tog, yo; rep from * to last 1 or 2 sts, knit to end.

NEXT ROW: Sl 1, knit to end.

Rep last row once more.

BO.

Join yarn to sts rem on needle and complete as for first side.

SLEEVES (MAKE 2)

Once you are done with the body, return to the sleeves. Place the held sts onto shorter circular needle or DPNs. Join for working in the rnd.

Work in est mesh patt for about 1½" (4cm), or desired length.

BO loosely.

FINISHING

Weave in ends.

Cord

With crochet hook, crochet a 30" (76cm) chain. Weave chain through eyelet neck edge.

To keep the integrity of the mesh pattern on the sleeves, each sleeve needs to have an even number of stitches. Adjust your marker placement as necessary to achieve an even number.

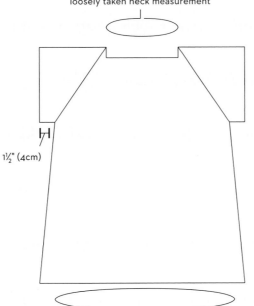

loosely taken neck measurement

1½" (4cm)

length from shoulder to hip bone, or as desired

bust measurement + 1-2" (3-5cm)

Little Darlings

Patterns for Babies and Kids

Yes, it's a cliché, but knitting for children is a total joy, mostly because the pint-sized sweaters take a tenth of the time as the adult-sized sweaters (OK, we're exaggerating). Knitchicks highly recommend that beginners take on a Little Darlings project as their first project because it will go quickly and will always be most satisfying—particularly when you give it to the parent of a Little Darling.

Baby Diamond

The Knitchicks love making baby clothes! The excitement and anticipation of a whole new person are knitted into every stitch. This cute pattern by Helen Stewart looks delicate and intricate, but it is not at all difficult—and it will be treasured by the new parents!

Pauline

FINISHED SIZES
To fit 0–3 (3–6, 9–12) months

FINISHED MEASUREMENTS
Chest: 16 (20½, 22¾)" (41 [52, 58]cm)
Length from shoulder: 10½ (12, 13½)" (27 [31, 34]cm)

YARN
2 (2, 2) skeins Grignasco Bambi (100% extrafine merino wool, 245yds [224m] per 50g skein)
color 185 light green

NEEDLES
16" (40cm) size US 4 (3.5mm) circular needle
16" (40cm) size US 3 (3.25mm) circular needle
size US 4 (3.5mm) DPNs
size US 3 (3.25mm) DPNs

NOTIONS
4 removable stitch markers
1 regular stitch marker
1 button

GAUGE
28 sts and 38 rows = 4" (10cm) in St st with larger needles

NOTES
pm (place marker): Slip a premade marker or a loosely knotted piece of scrap yarn in a contrasting color onto the right needle after the st just knit to mark a spot in the knitting to refer to on future rows. When you come to a marker, simply slip it from the left-hand needle to the right-hand needle.

Sl marker or sl st(s) (slip marker or slip stitch[es]): Slip a st or sts purlwise from the left needle to the right needle. When slipping a marker, knit the sts before and after it as usual.

yo (yarn over): Wrap the working yarn around the needle and knit the next st as usual. This operation creates an eyelet hole in the knitting and inc 1 st.

k2tog (knit 2 together): Dec 1 st by knitting 2 sts tog.

SSK (slip, slip, knit): Dec 1 st by slipping 2 sts knitwise 1 at a time, inserting the tip of the left needle into both sts and knitting the 2 sts tog.

psso (pass slipped stitch over): When instructed to knit 1, slip 1, the pattern may then tell you to pass the slipped st over the st just knit, dec 1 st. Simply follow the pattern as written, passing the slipped st over any previous st(s) as indicated.

YOKE

With smaller circular needle, CO 76 (88, 92) sts. Do not join.

ROWS 1–6: Knit.

Change to larger circular needle.

ROW 7 (RS): Pm for raglan shaping as foll: K12 (14, 15) for left front, yo, k1, place removable marker in st just knit, yo, k12 (14, 14) for left sleeve, yo, k1, pm in st just knit, yo, k24 (28, 30) for back, yo, k1, pm in st just knit, yo, k12 (14, 14) for right sleeve, yo, k1, pm in st just knit, yo, k12 (14, 15) for right front—84 (96, 100) sts.

Note: You should have 4 marked sts with yarn overs on either side.

ROW 8: K3, purl to last 3 sts, k3.

ROW 9: *Knit to first marker, yo, knit to next marker, yo; rep from * 3 times more, knit to end—8 sts inc.

Rep Rows 8–9 13 (18, 21) times more, then Row 8 only once—196 (248, 276) sts.

SEPARATE BODY AND SLEEVES

NEXT ROW (RS): Removing markers as you come to them, k28 (35, 39) sts, place next 42 (54, 60) sts on holder, use backward-loop method (see page 19) to CO 0 (2, 2) sts for underarm, k56 (70, 78) sts, place next 42 (54, 60) sts on holder, CO 0 (2, 2) sts for underarm, k28 (35, 39) sts—112 (144, 160) sts rem on needle.

Join for working in the rnd. K28 (36, 40) sts, pm at underarm. This is the beg of the rnd from now on.

BODY

Work in St st until Body measures 2¾ (3½, 4¼)" (7 [9, 11]cm) from underarm.

Work Rnds 1–17 of Diamond Lace Chart. Note that on Rnd 7 only, you will need to shift the beg of the rnd back by 1 st to accommodate the first sl 1-k2tog-psso.

After chart is complete, work 4 rnds even in St st.

Change to smaller circular needle and work 8 rnds in garter st (knit and purl alternate rnds).

BO loosely.

SLEEVES (MAKE 2)

Place 42 (54, 60) held sts on larger DPNs. Pick up and k 1 st from underarm, pm for beg of rnd, pick up and k 1 st—44 (56, 62) sts.

Work 6 rnds even in St st.

NEXT RND: K1, k2tog, knit to last 3 sts, SSK, k1—2 sts dec.

Rep last 7 rnds 4 (5, 6) times more—34 (44, 48) sts.

Work 6 (6, 3) rnds even.

Change to smaller DPNs and work in garter st for 6 rnds.

BO loosely.

FINISHING

Weave in ends. Block. Make button loop at top of neck opening and sew on button opposite.

The yoke is knit back and forth to create the neck placket opening, and then the remainder of the sweater is worked in the round.

Diamond Lace Chart

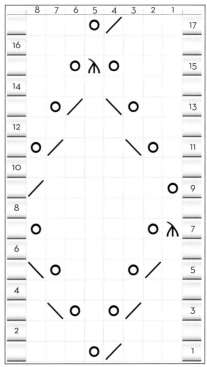

Legend

☐	Knit	╲	ssk
╱	k2tog	人	sl k2tog psso
O	yo		

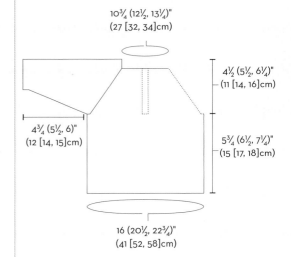

10¾ (12½, 13¼)"
(27 [32, 34]cm)

4½ (5½, 6¼)"
(11 [14, 16]cm)

4¾ (5½, 6)"
(12 [14, 15]cm)

5¾ (6½, 7¼)"
(15 [17, 18]cm)

16 (20½, 22¾)"
(41 [52, 58]cm)

Jarrah

I struggle a lot with intarsia because I didn't learn the technique correctly. Plus, I have this nagging insistence on knitting in the round, which traditional intarsia resents. I created Jarrah for the anti-intarsia in me. I wanted to give my daughter a stripy top that had some pizzazz to it, while still working in the round.

Marcelle

FINISHED MEASUREMENTS

Chest: 22–24 (26–28, 30–32)" (56–61 [66–71, 76–82]cm)
Length from shoulder: 17" (43cm)

FIT

Standard

YARN

3 skeins Rowan All Season Cotton (60% cotton, 40% acrylic, 98 yds [90m] per 50g skein)
  color #185 Jazz (blue)
2 skeins Rowan All Season Cotton (60% cotton, 40% acrylic, 98 yds [90m] per 50g skein)
  color #203 Giddy (purple)

NEEDLES

24" (60cm) size US 7 (4.5mm) circular needle
size US 5 (3.75mm) DPNs (for tighter-fitting sleeves)
or size US 7 (4.5mm) DPNs

NOTIONS

4 stitch markers
2 stitch holders
tapestry needle

GAUGE

16 sts and 23 rows = 4" (10cm) in St st with larger needle

NOTES

pm (place marker): Slip a premade marker or a loosely knotted piece of scrap yarn in a contrasting color onto the right needle after the st just knit to mark a spot in the knitting to refer to on future rows. When you come to a marker, simply slip it from the left-hand needle to the right-hand needle.

Sl marker or sl st(s) (slip marker or slip stitch[es]): Slip a st or sts purlwise from the left needle to the right needle. When slipping a marker, knit the sts before and after it as usual.

KFB (knit 1 front and back): Inc 1 st by knitting into the front and back of the next st, creating 2 new sts on right-hand needle.

k2tog (knit 2 together): Dec 1 st by knitting 2 sts tog.

SSK (slip, slip, knit): Dec 1 st by slipping 2 sts knitwise 1 at a time, inserting the tip of the left needle into both sts and knitting the 2 sts tog.

Before You Begin

You'll be knitting this lightweight, every-season-but-winter jumper from the top down. Here we're going for a square neck, short raglan sleeves and a loose-fitting body. There's optional shaping for those who want a closer fit. And don't forget to measure your child!

YOKE

Using a circular needle and color A, CO approx 64 (74, 80) sts. Pm and join for working in the rnd.

Work in k1, p1 rib for 1" (3cm).

SEPARATE BODY AND SLEEVES

Now you'll divide the sts on the needle into back, front and sleeves and pm for the raglan yoke inc. Remember your rule of 3? It works here: ⅓ of total sts for back, ⅓ for front, ⅓ for sleeves. So, if you have 64 sts, knit 22 for the back, pm, knit 10 for a sleeve, pm, knit 22 for the front, pm, and finally knit 10 for the other sleeve.

On the next rnd, start inc as foll: *KFB, knit to 1 st before next marker, KFB, sl marker; rep from * to end of rnd—8 sts inc.

Cont to inc as est on every other rnd until you have enough sts in the back and front sections put together to fit comfortably around the child's chest.

Make sure the length of the raglan (the diagonal increase line) is long enough as well. Add a few more rnds if necessary.

BODY

Transfer the sleeve sts to holders and knit the body as foll: On the next rnd, knit across the back sts to the marker. Remove the marker and place sleeve sts on a holder. Sl the next marker to the right-hand needle. Knit across the front sts to the third marker, remove it and place the second set of sleeve sts on another holder. Leave the beg-of-rnd marker in place.

You should have the front and back sts united on the needle, with 1 marker at each underarm.

Knit straight, changing colors as desired, until the sweater is about ½" (1cm) short of the total desired length.

Knit 1 row, purl 1 row, knit 1 row.

BO loosely.

SLEEVES (MAKE 2)

Transfer first set of sleeve sts to DPNs, distributing them evenly. Pm at underarm. Join for working in the rnd, keeping stripe sequence as est.

Knit approx 6 rnds even. If desired, knit more or fewer rnds here for desired sleeve length.

Knit 1 row, purl 1 row, knit 1 row.

BO loosely.

FINISHING

Weave in ends and block.

Remember to keep your cast on loose! These cast-on numbers are only guides. They are equivalent to a collar circumference of 16 (18½, 20)" (41 [47, 51]cm). Measure your child and cast on more or fewer stitches as necessary.

*Rib: *K1, p1; rep from * to end.*

Because you will need three additional stitch markers when you begin the yoke shaping, the first one placed should be a different color than the other three to clearly mark the beginning of a round.

The Stripes:
*Once you have knit approx 4–5" (10–13cm) in color A, begin stripe sequence as foll: *K1 color A, k1 color B; rep from * to end. Rep this rnd once more, then cut yarn A and cont with B only for 9 more rnds. Switch back to A as foll: *K1 color B, k1 color A; rep from * to end. Rep this rnd once more, then cut yarn B and cont with A only for 9 more rnds. Keep alternating A and B in this manner for the rest of the sweater.*

Optional Shaping:
If you want, you may create a boxy neckline for the sweater by working intermittent increases and decreases.
  *Dec at underarms on every 4th rnd as foll: *SSK, knit to 2 sts before marker, k2tog, sl marker; rep from * once more.*
  Each decrease round subtracts 1" (3cm) from the chest circumference. Work as many decrease rounds as you like.

The bottom hem is garter stitch. How do you do garter in the round? You knit one row, you purl the next!

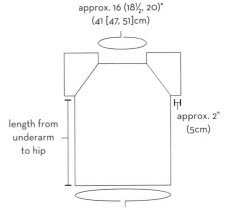

approx. 16 (18½, 20)"
(41 [47, 51]cm)

approx. 2" (5cm)

length from underarm to hip

chest measurement + 1½–3" (4–8cm)

Kaia

Maren Waxenberg is one of my dearest and most talented crafty friends. When she first showed me "her" steeking technique, I knew (a) She was a Knitchick extraordinaire and (b) I had to ask her for a few of her designs to feature in this book.

Maren learned to knit in Norway from a Norwegian friend. When she returned to the States, she couldn't find a knitting community and so had to discover some things on her own. She dissected a Norwegian ski sweater a great aunt had given her and found that the sleeves were sewn in place. Maren describes it as a "glorious click moment" because she realized she could knit all the sweater pieces as tubes and then sew them together at the end.

We know the idea of cutting into your knitting can be scary, but if you consider the work just another piece of fabric, it becomes a simple sewing project. If you're really nervous, experiment cutting through a knit swatch until you've got the hang of it.

Marcelle

A Special Touch

Maren's daughter Kaia designed the flowers embroidered onto the bodice of this sweater. You can use her design, or use a pretty drawing from the little one in your life.

FINISHED MEASUREMENTS

Measure the child's chest and add 3–4" (8–10cm) for ease.
For example, the sample as shown was knit for a 7-year-old girl.
Sample measurements:
Chest: 28½" (72cm)
Length from shoulder: 16" (41cm)

FIT
Standard to Loose

YARN
2 skeins of Blue Sky Alpacas Royal Alpaca (100% royal alpaca, 288yds [263m] per 100g skein) in the foll colors:
color 707 Patina (A)
color 708 Seaglass (B)
color 700 Alabaster (C)

NEEDLES
16" and 24" (40cm and 60cm) size US 2 (2.75mm) circular needles
size US 2 (2.75mm) DPNs

NOTIONS
stitch markers
tapestry needle
sewing machine
crochet hook
3 buttons

GAUGE
28 sts and 40 rows = 4" (10cm) in St st

NOTES

pm (place marker): Slip a premade marker or a loosely knotted piece of scrap yarn in a contrasting color onto the right needle after the st just knit to mark a spot in the knitting to refer to on future rows. When you come to a marker, simply slip it from the left-hand needle to the right-hand needle.

SSK (slip, slip, knit): Dec 1 st by slipping 2 sts knitwise 1 at a time, inserting the tip of the left needle into both sts and knitting the 2 sts tog.

Sl marker or sl st(s) (slip marker or slip stitch[es]): Sl a st or sts purlwise from the left needle to the right needle. When slipping a marker, knit the sts before and after it as usual.

k2tog (knit 2 together): Dec 1 st by knitting 2 sts tog.

BODY

With color A and using the longer circular needle, CO the number of sts required for your chest size plus 3–4" (8–10cm) for ease. Pm and join for working in the rnd. Work in St st for 1" (3cm).

Purl 1 rnd.

Cont in St st until work measures 5" (13cm) from purl rnd, or desired length.

Change to color C and work even until piece measures desired body length from purl rnd.

Purl 1 rnd. (This will become the fold line for the neckline hem.)

Work even in St st for 1" (3cm).

BO.

The body is worked as a tube on circular needles, straight up from hem to neck. Make the tube before you do any other part. It is your foundation. No holes are left for the sleeves because they will be cut and set in using a sewing machine.

The first 1" (3cm) plus the purl round will become the bottom hem. You are creating the fold line for your hem.

For smaller sizes, the color A section can be a little shorter, and for larger sizes it can be taller. Whatever proportion looks right to you is fine. The bit worked in color C is where you'll be embroidering your flower! Measure from the top of the shoulder to the hip bone (or lower) to find the body length.

SLEEVES (MAKE 2)

With color B and shorter circular needle, CO the number of sts required for the top of the sleeve. Pm and join for working in the rnd.

Work in reverse St st (purl every rnd) for 1" (3cm).

Change to St st (knit every rnd) and work even until sleeve measures approx half of total desired length to cuff from last purl rnd.

Begin dec as foll: Knit to 3 sts before marker, SSK, k1, sl marker, k2, k2tog. Rep dec as est on every 3rd rnd until sleeve is desired length minus 4" (10cm) for cuff.

The sleeves are knit from the top down to the cuff. To find the number of stitches for the top of the sleeve, add 1" (3cm) for ease to your armhole depth, multiply that number by 2, then multiply by the gauge (7 sts per inch or 2.8 sts per cm). If your armhole depth is 6" (15cm), that's 7 x 2 x 7 = 98 sts to cast on. To measure armhole depth, measure straight down from the top of the shoulder to the underarm.

The reverse Stockinette stitch portion will become the facing when using the sewing machine to attach the sleeves.

When your sleeve becomes too narrow to continue on the circular, switch to double-pointed needles.

CUFF

RND 1: *K3, p3; rep from * to end.

Rep Rnd 1 for 4" (10cm).

BO loosely.

The cuff will measure 4" (10cm), unfolded, so allow for this length in your calculations. The cuff requires a multiple of 6 stitches. You can adjust the stitch count, if necessary, right before the cuff by decreasing an extra stitch or two, or you can use a different ribbing, such as k2, p2 (multiple of 4 sts).

FINISHING

With the sweater inside out, sew the facings invisibly around the sleeve seam to hide the rough edges. Avoid pulling the sewing thread to keep the fabric from puckering. Sew down the facing around the neckline. Then handsew the right shoulder seam and prepare the left shoulder seam for buttons. Turn sweater RS out.

Embroidered Embellishments

Involve the child you are knitting the sweater for in the design process. Have the child draw a simple picture of a flower garden or another simple design and embroider the drawing onto the front of the sweater using yarn, embroidery thread, ribbon, beads and so on. Embroider the design in duplicate stitch so it looks as if it were knit into the work.

Fringe

Cut scraps and ends from the embroidery into 5–6" (13–15cm) pieces, then fold them in half. Use a crochet hook to bring the folded loop through the purled hem stitch and then pull the fringe ends through the loop in a lark's head knot.

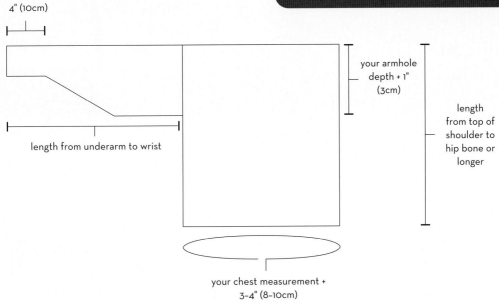

4" (10cm)

length from underarm to wrist

your armhole depth + 1" (3cm)

length from top of shoulder to hip bone or longer

your chest measurement + 3–4" (8–10cm)

Norwegian Steeking Technique

Norwegian sweaters are traditionally knit in the round. After the body tube is completed, the armholes are cut open and the sleeves (also knit as tubes) are sewn in. Although many knitters might be afraid to cut their work, thinking of the knitting as a piece of fabric to be sewn makes it easier. The following is a step-by-step tutorial of the steeking process. This technique is especially suited to knitters who are comfortable sewing with a sewing machine.

The steeking process creates a strong, stable sleeve line in the sweater and saves time because all elements of the sweater are knit in the round. The inside of the sweater is neat, attractive and finished-looking as well.

1. MARK ARMHOLE PLACEMENT

Mark the top of each side seam with a straight pin. Position a finished sleeve where it should be attached to the sweater body, with the top of the sleeve at the point where the facing begins to get its height. Now mark the armhole depth on the bodice by placing a pin at the point where the sleeve will end. Put another pin in the same spot on the other side.

2. REINFORCE THE ARMHOLE WITH STITCHING

Set your sewing machine to a tight straight or a very narrow zigzag stitch, and sew a reinforcing seam on the bodice where the sleeves will be inset. Starting at the top of the sweater, stitch down to the pin you placed at the sleeve depth, turn and stitch at a right angle over 4 knit stitches, turn again and sew back up to the top of the sweater. You will create a stitched area roughly the shape of an elongated "U" from the neckline down to the point where the sleeve will end. Go over the same stitching line again so you have double-stitching around the armhole. Note: You may find it helpful to use regular sewing thread in a slightly contrasting color so you can easily see the sewing-machine stitch against the knitted work. Repeat this process on the other side for the other armhole.

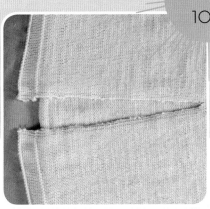

3. CUT ARMHOLES

Prepare to cut the work with sharp scissors. Place a pin at the point where the armhole ends. This is the point at the base of the elongated "U" where you turned the work to begin stitching up the other side. The pin will stop the scissors from cutting too far. Beginning at the top of the work, between the 2 stitched sides (or down the middle of the stitched "U"), carefully cut the length of the armhole. Don't worry about unraveling because you have secured the work with the machine stitching. Do not at any point cut across the machine stitching. Repeat for the second armhole.

4. STITCH AROUND ARMHOLE

With Right Sides together, reattach the top of the armhole at the facing edge with a ½" (1cm) machine seam. This creates the armhole into which you will sew the sleeve.

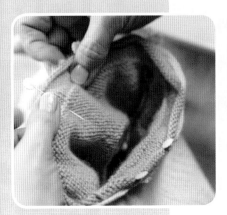

5. SEAM SLEEVES INTO ARMHOLES

With Right Sides together, set the first sleeve into the armhole and pin it in place. Remember the facings on both the sleeve and the bodice go to the inside. Sew the sleeve in place with a regular machine seam. Go around the same stitching line again to reinforce the sleeve seam. Repeat for the remaining sleeve.

Oscar

Cables look so much more difficult than they actually are. This pattern will introduce you to the basic concept of how to create that "twisted" look with a single cable up the middle of the vest.

Knitting on big needles with chunky wool, you'll speed through this in no time.

Pauline

FINISHED SIZES
1 (2) years

FINISHED MEASUREMENTS
Chest: 21 (23½)" (53 [60]cm)
Length: 10¼ (12¾)" (26 [32]cm)

YARN
1 (2) skeins Misti International Misti Alpaca Chunky (100% alpaca; 108yds [99m] per 100g skein)

color M707 Copper Melange

NEEDLES
size US 10½ (6.5mm) straight needles

NOTIONS
stitch holders
spare knitting needle for three-needle bind off
tapestry needle
cable needle

GAUGE
13 sts and 16 rows = 4" (10cm) in St st

NOTES
SSK (slip, slip, knit): Dec 1 st by slipping 2 sts knitwise 1 at a time, inserting the tip of the left needle into both sts and knitting the 2 sts tog.

k2tog (knit 2 together): Dec 1 st by knitting 2 sts tog.

Sl (slip): Slip a st from the left needle to the right needle knitwise on RS rows, purlwise on WS rows.

C6F (cable 6 front): Slip 3 sts onto a cable needle and hold them to the front of the work. Knit 3 sts from the left-hand needle. Knit the 3 sts from the cable needle. The 6 refers to the total number of sts involved in the cable, and the F instructs you to hold the sts to the front of the work. See page 111 for complete step-by-step instructions.

FRONT

CO 36 (40) sts.

ROW 1 (RS): K1 (3), *p2, k2; rep from * to last 3 (5) sts, p2, k1 (3).

ROW 2 (WS): P1 (3), *k2, p2; rep from * to last 3 (5) sts, k2, p1 (3).

ROWS 3–4: Rep Rows 1–2.

ROW 5: K13 (15), (p2, k2) twice, p2, k13 (15).

ROW 6: P13 (15), (k2, p2) twice, k2, p13 (15).

ROWS 7–8: Rep Rows 5–6.

ROW 9: K13 (15), p2, C6F, p2, k13 (15).

ROWS 10, 12, 14 AND 16: P13 (15), k2, p6, k2, p13 (15).

ROWS 11, 13 AND 15: K13 (15), p2, k6, p2, k13 (15).

Rep Rows 9–16 1 (2) times more.

NEXT ROW (RS): Rep Row 9.

Neck and Armhole Shaping

NEXT ROW (WS): BO 2 sts, purl 10 (12) sts, (k2, p2) twice, k2, p13 (15).

NEXT ROW (RS): BO 2 sts, k1, SSK, k4 (5), k2tog, k1, p2, k3. Turn—14 (16) sts. Place rem sts on holder.

NEXT ROW: Sl 1, p2, k2, p to end.

NEXT ROW: Sl 1, k1, SSK, knit to last 8 sts, k2tog, k1, p2, k3—12 (14) sts.

NEXT ROW: Sl 1, p2, k2, purl to end.

NEXT ROW: Sl 1, knit to last 8 sts, k2tog, k1, p2, k3—11 (13) sts.

Rep last 2 rows 3 (4) times more—8 (9) sts.

NEXT ROW: Sl 1, p2, k2, purl to end.

NEXT ROW: Sl 1, k2 (3), p2, k3.

Rep last 2 rows until armhole measures 4 (4½)" (10 [11]cm).

Place sts on a second holder and cut yarn, leaving a 12" (30cm) tail. Replace sts from first holder on needle. With RS of work facing you, join yarn.

NEXT ROW (RS): Sl 1, k2, p2, k1, SSK, knit to last 5 sts, k2tog, k2—14 (16) sts.

NEXT ROW (WS): Sl 1, purl to last 5 sts, k2, p3.

Rep last 2 rows once more—12 (14) sts.

NEXT ROW: Sl 1, k2, p2, k1, SSK, knit to end—11 (13) sts.

NEXT ROW: Sl 1, p to last 5 sts, k2, p3.

Rep last 2 rows 3 (4) times more—8 (9) sts.

NEXT ROW: Sl 1, p2, k2, purl to end.

NEXT ROW: Sl 1, k2 (3), p2, k3.

Rep last 2 rows until armhole measures 4 (4½)" (10 [11]cm). Place sts on a holder and cut yarn, leaving a 12" (30cm) tail.

Rows 1–4 make up the bottom ribbing.

Rows 5–8 are the cable set-up rows.

This section is the cable pattern repeat.

Slipping the first stitch of each row ensures a smooth edge. To do this on an Right Side (knit) row, place your needle in the next stitch as if to knit it, but instead slip it to the right needle. On the Wrong Side (purl) rows, place your needle in the next stitch as if to purl it, but instead slip it to the right needle.

Now to the other side: Start working this side from the middle. To join the yarn, simply hold the yarn as normal (leaving a tail) and start knitting. It might feel odd as it's not attached to anything, but it soon will be!

BACK

CO 36 (40) sts.

Row 1 (RS): K1 (3), *p2, k2; rep from * to last 3 (5) sts, p2, k1 (3).

Row 2 (WS): P1 (3), *k2, p2; rep from * to last 3 (5) sts, k2, p1 (3).

Rows 3–4: Rep Rows 1–2.

Change to St st, beg with a knit row. Work even for 21 (29) rows.

Next Row (WS): BO 2 sts, purl to end.

Next Row (RS): BO 2 sts, k1, SSK, knit to last 4 sts, k2tog, k2—30 (34) sts.

Next Row: Sl 1, purl to end.

Next Row: Sl 1, k1, SSK, knit to last 4 sts, k2tog, k2—28 (32) sts.

Next Row: Sl 1, purl to end.

Next Row: Sl 1, knit to end.

Rep last 2 rows until armhole measures 4 (4½)" (10 [11]cm). Leave sts on needle. Do not cut yarn.

FINISHING

There are now 2 complete pieces (not yet bound off) with the back stitches on 1 needle and the front sts on holders. Move all the front sts to the second needle.

To complete the vest, bind off the 8 (9) shoulder sts using the three needle bind-off method as foll:

Step 1: Hold the front and back pieces tog with RS facing and needles parallel.

Step 2: Insert the spare (third) needle into the first st on the front needle as if to knit, then into the first st on the back needle. Knit these 2 sts tog as if they were 1 st.

Step 3: Rep Step 2 with the next st on each needle.

Step 4: Bind off 1 st by passing the first st on the right-hand needle over the second and off the needle.

Rep Steps 3–4 to bind off the 8 (9) sts of the first shoulder.

Cont binding off in the normal way across 12 (14) back neck sts, until 8 (9) sts rem for second shoulder.

BO second shoulder same as first.

Block the piece by steaming gently. Sew up the side seams. Weave in ends.

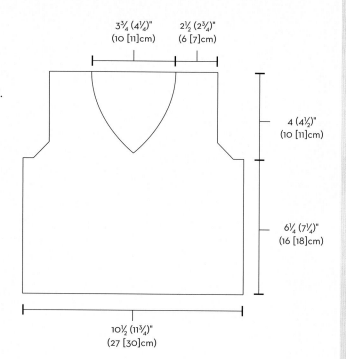

3¾ (4¼)" (10 [11]cm) 2½ (2¾)" (6 [7]cm)

4 (4½)" (10 [11]cm)

6¼ (7¼)" (16 [18]cm)

10½ (11¾)" (27 [30]cm)

Knitting Cables

Cables are achieved by moving the order of the stitches around on the needles. A special cable needle helps you perform this technique.

      The instructions in this pattern are for C6F—cable six stitches forward. This means six stitches will be cabled: Half of that number (three) are slid onto the cable needle and held to the front of the work (hence the "F" in C6F), while the other three are knitted as usual.

      If the instructions had read C6B, the cable needle and stitches would be held to the back and the cable would "twist" in the other direction.

1. PLACE STITCHES ON CABLE NEEDLE

Place the next 3 stitches onto a cable needle and hold to the front of your work.

2. KNIT STITCHES

Ignoring those on the cable needle, knit the next 3 stitches (you will need to stretch the stitches a bit).

3. KNIT STITCHES ON CABLE NEEDLE

Knit the 3 stitches from the cable needle.

Ruby Ruffle

Newsflash: I *love* making things for my daughter Ruby. When she was a baby, I made dozens of *Aviva* sweaters (see page 122) for her. As she's gotten older, I've expanded my repertoire. I ended up designing the *Ruby Ruffle* based on the "puffy shirt" from *Seinfeld*. I wanted something as elaborate as that memorable garment, but cooler, of course. I'm really pleased with this one—and so is Ruby.

Marcelle

Helpful Hint

Any comfortable, lightweight cotton will work for this top. I chose the Sierra Quatro because it has a nice stiffness to it, which I wanted for the ruffle bit. The other really amazing thing about the Sierra Quatro line is you get a lot of yardage for your buck. I used only two skeins for my then seven-year-old daughter.

FINISHED MEASUREMENTS

Measure the child's chest and add 1–2" (3–5cm) for ease.
For example, the sample as shown was knit for a 7-year-old girl.
Sample measurements:
Chest: 26" (66cm)
Length from shoulder: 17½" (45cm)

FIT

Close

YARN

2 skeins Cascade Yarns Sierra Quatro (85% pima cotton, 15% merino wool, 191yds [175m] per 100g skein)
color 86 pink-red-purple twist

NEEDLES

24" (60cm) size US 7 (4.5mm) circular needle
size US 5 (3.75mm) DPNs

NOTIONS

stitch markers
stitch holders
tapestry needle

GAUGE

17 sts and 23 rows = 4" (10cm) in St st with larger needles

NOTES

pm (place marker): Slip a premade marker or a loosely knotted piece of scrap yarn in a contrasting color onto the right needle after the st just knit to mark a spot in the knitting to refer to on future rows. When you come to a marker, simply slip it from the right-hand needle to the left-hand needle.

k2tog (knit 2 together): Dec 1 st by knitting 2 sts tog.

yo (yarn over): Wrap the working yarn around the needle and knit the next st as usual. This operation creates an eyelet hole in the knitting and inc 1 st.

M1 (make 1): Inc 1 st by picking up the bar between the next st and the st just knit and knitting into it.

KFB (knit 1 front and back): Inc 1 st by knitting into the next st, and without sliding the st off the left-hand needle, knitting into the back of the same st. Slide old st off left-hand needle, creating 2 new sts on right-hand needle.

PICOT EDGING

With a circular needle, CO the number of sts needed for your chest measurement plus 1–2" (3–5cm). Pm and join for working in the rnd.

Knit 3 rnds.

EYELET RND: *K2tog, yo; rep from * around.

Knit 2 rnds.

PICOT RND: Now it gets interesting. Fold the hem inward, toward the Wrong Side. You are folding at the yarn-over perforations, as it were.

Pick up 1 st from the outside of the cast-on edge and k2tog—your second st is already on your left-hand needle. How do you know you've achieved picot? You've got this cute little V dangling.

Cont to work 1 rnd in picot. This rnd only happens once, so when you're done, you're ready to knit St st to the underarm. As you work this rnd, pm at the second side seam.

BODY

Here's where you cruise for about 13" (33cm), or desired length. Knit plain in St st until the body is your desired length. Place the 8 sts to the side of each marker on holders. That's 16 sts each on 2 holders, directly opposite each other. (You can remove the markers now.) The working yarn should be right behind 1 of those sets of 16 sts, ready to knit across them. Don't cut the yarn.

Use the long-tail method (see pages 20–21) and cast on loosely.

The picot edge is a favorite hem of mine, but it is quite tricky as you need to align your stitches just so.

Where are you folding? At the eyelet row. Use that row as your hemline.

The secret? The stitch you are picking up has to be directly aligned with the stitch on your needle.

Placing a second stitch marker at the halfway point of the round will help you place the sleeves.

Before You Begin

This pattern is worked in the round from the bottom up with a picot edge. The picot-edge short sleeves are knit onto the garment and require a simple Kitchener stitch to keep it all together. The neck shaping is all about the rapid decrease, and the ruffle is simply created by picking up stitches around the neck. It's really very little effort for very nice results.

SLEEVES (MAKE 2)

With DPNs, CO enough sts to go around the upper arm, plus 1" (3cm) for ease. Join for working in the rnd. Work your picot edge the same as on the body.

Work approx 10 rnds even.

INC ROW: K1, M1, knit to last st, M1, k1—2 sts inc.

Work the inc a total of 5 times—10 sts inc.

Knit even for 4 rnds.

Place the last 8 and the first 8 sts of the rnd on a holder.

The Seamless Sleeve

The seamless sleeve is a work of magic, but it's a bit of work.

Take up the circular needle holding the body sts. Now knit the sts of 1 sleeve onto the circular needle. When all the sleeve sts are knit on, cont to knit across the body, skipping the 16 sts on the holder. When you get to the second holder, knit the other sleeve sts onto the circular needle in the same way as the first, then cont knitting across the body sts. When you finish, you should have a body tube with 2 sleeve tubes attached at either side.

YOKE

This is where the shaping begins. Work in St st for 1" (3cm) or more, basically to get comfortable.

Scoop Neck

Now you'll work a rapid dec here to reduce the neckline by nearly half.

DEC ROW: *K2, k2tog; rep from * around.

Knit 3 rnds even.

Rep Dec Row.

You should end up with roughly 55% the number of sts you had before, but don't stress over this number.

Once you've done the rapid dec, knit another 1" (3cm) or more, until the yoke is deep enough for your taste.

Bind off. You now have a nice open scoop neck.

Ruffly Edge

Turn the top inside out. With the Wrong Side facing you, pick up and knit 1 st in every bound-off st around the neck. Pm and join for working in the rnd.

Knit 1 rnd even.

On the next rnd, double the number of sts by working KFB in every st.

NEXT ROW: Work in *K1, p1; rep from * around.

Cont in rib for 5 more rnds.

BO.

FINISHING

Use Kitchener stitch to graft the underarm sts together (see pages 32–33). Weave in ends.

Why are you going down 2 needle sizes for the sleeves? I prefer to do so as it makes the sleeves more snug than the body part.

You can adjust the length of the sleeves here. The sleeves on the sweater shown are about 6" (15cm) long.

These 16 sts will be joined with 16 sts from the body at the underarm.

You want to knit about ½ the total depth of the yoke here.

Helpful Hint
You could make this top for the adult woman in your life as well just by adjusting your measurements.

length from underarm to hip, or longer

upper arm +1" (3cm)

chest measurement + 1–2" (3–5cm)

Ruby's Cami

I've always wanted to wear tube tops and tanks with spaghetti straps, but my boobs got in the way, even when I was pretty young. So now I'm making all kinds of summery, easy-breezy tops for Ruby for those starry nights on the beaches of Fire Island.

After I knit *Ruby's Cami*, I had enough yarn left over to make a matching shrug (see page 120). Sometimes overbuying leads to some really nice results.

Marcelle

FINISHED MEASUREMENTS

Measure the child's chest and do not add room for ease.
For example, the sample as shown was knit for a 6-year-old girl.
Sample measurements:
Chest: 22½" (57cm)
Length from shoulder: 19½" (50cm)

FIT

Very close

YARN

2 skeins of Blue Sky Alpacas Dyed Cotton (100% organic cotton, 150yds [137m] per 100g skein)
    color 631 Circus Peanut (MC)
1 skein of Blue Sky Alpacas Dyed Cotton (100% organic cotton, 150yds [137m] per 100g skein) in each of the foll colors:
    color 618 Orchid (CC1)
    color 604 Aloe (CC2)

NEEDLES

24" (60cm) size US 8 (5mm) circular needle

NOTIONS

stitch markers
removable markers or pins
tapestry needle
crochet hook (optional)

GAUGE

17 sts and 20 rows = 4" (10cm) in St st
16 sts and 21 rows = 4" (10cm) in 2-Color Broken Rib

NOTES

yo (yarn over): Wrap the working yarn around the needle and knit the next st as usual. This operation creates an eyelet hole in the knitting and inc 1 st.

pm (place marker): Slip a premade marker or a loosely knotted piece of scrap yarn in a contrasting color onto the right needle after the st just knit to mark a spot in the knitting to refer to on future rows. When you come to a marker, simply slip it from the right-hand needle to the left-hand needle.

Sl marker or sl st(s) (slip marker or slip stitch[es]): Slip a st or sts purlwise from the left needle to the right needle. When slipping a marker, knit the sts before and after it as usual.

k2tog (knit 2 together): Dec 1 st by knitting 2 sts tog.

M1 (make 1): Inc 1 st by picking up the bar between the next st and the st just knit and knitting into it.

BODICE

With MC, CO enough sts to fit closely around the chest—96 sts for sample. Pm and join for working in the rnd. Cut MC and join CC1 and CC2.

The bodice should fit with little or no ease. Remember to calculate your cast-on number using the gauge for broken rib, not St st.

Broken Rib Section

Rnd 1: *K1 CC1, p1 CC2; rep from * to end.

Rnd 2: *K1 CC1, k1 CC2; rep from * to end.

You'll need an even number of sts to work the broken rib pattern.

Rep Rnds 1–2 for 5" (13cm), or desired bodice length.

Change to MC. Knit 1 rnd.

5" (13cm) is Ruby's measurement. Your child may have a shorter upper body or a longer one. The key is to measure. Once you are done with the two-tone colors, cut off a nice long tail that will be sewn into the body of the fabric later.

Next Rnd: *K2tog, yo; rep from * to end.

Knit 3 rnds even.

You are doing a transition here. I like to mark the transition with some lace-type stitch. In this case, we're going with yarn over.

SKIRT WITH OPEN BACK

At the end of the last rnd, remove marker, turn work and begin knitting back and forth in St st.

The beauty of this cami is that the back is open. You don't have to open the back. If you prefer a closed back, all you need to do is knit in the round until the cami reaches the bottom of the hip bone.

Row 1 (WS): K4, purl to last 4 sts placing 8 markers evenly spaced, k4.

Row 2 (RS): P4, knit to last 4 sts, p4.

Row 3: K4, purl to last 4 sts, k4.

Row 4: P4, *knit to marker, sl marker, M1; rep from * 7 times more, knit to last 4 sts, p4—8 sts inc.

You'll need a border to keep the open back edges from curling in. We did a checkered pattern. The markers show where you'll increase to make the skirt flare out. How do you space your markers evenly? Take the number of sts on your needles, subtract 8 sts for the borders, and divide the result by 8. Place the markers that many stitches apart. Starting with 90 sts, that works out to a marker every 8 sts, with 2 stitches left over. Don't worry about extra stitches; just put them before the first marker and after the last marker.

Row 5: Rep Row 3.

Row 6: Rep Row 2.

Row 7: Purl.

Row 8: *Knit to marker, sl marker, M1; rep from * 7 times more, knit to end—8 sts inc.

Row 9: Purl.

Row 10: Knit.

Row 11: Purl.

ROW 12: Rep Row 8—8 sts inc.

ROWS 13, 15, 17: K4, purl to last 4 sts, k4.

ROWS 14, 16, 18: P4, knit to last 4 sts, p4.

ROWS 19, 21, 23: Purl.

ROWS 20, 22, 24: Knit.

Rep Rows 13–24 until skirt reaches the bottom of the hip bone, or to desired length less 1" (3cm).

Hem

Knit in garter st for 1" (3cm).

BO very, very loosely.

STRAPS

With MC, RS facing, pick up and knit 4 sts off the front where you've placed a marker. Knit in garter st, sl the first st of every row. Cont working in garter st until the strap measures 11" (28cm), or desired length.

BO.

FINISHING

Sew straps down in back at marked positions. Obviously, you need to sew up any loose strings, but then you're all done, and your child can go to the park in her new top.

Where do I place the straps? You need 4 points, 2 front and 2 back. Place the camisole on your child's body and use removable stitch markers or pins to mark where you want the straps to go. The straps will stretch some with wear, so err on the side of shorter rather than longer. The straps are knit in garter stitch and work up very quickly.

You can knit or crochet the straps, whatever your preference. The key is to measure the length of the strap before you fasten it onto the body of the top.

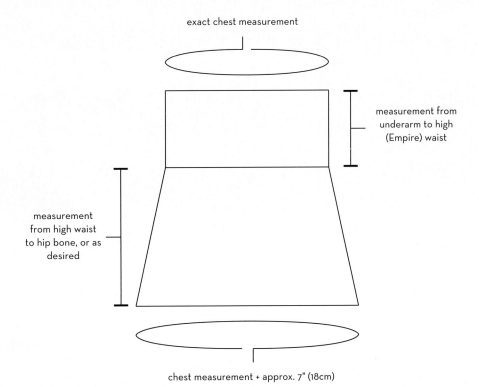

exact chest measurement

measurement from underarm to high (Empire) waist

measurement from high waist to hip bone, or as desired

chest measurement + approx. 7" (18cm)

Ruby's Shrug

I had left-over yarn. It kills me to have leftover yarn; it feels like a waste. Eyeballing what I had left over, I could see I didn't have enough for another top. So I opted for a short-sleeved, two-tone, no-button shrug. No buttons? I will sheepishly admit that I didn't have any on me when I began designing the shrug, and I will unabashedly admit that buttons are your choice for this shrug.

Marcelle

FINISHED MEASUREMENTS

Measure the child's chest and add 1" (3cm) for ease.
For example, the sample as shown was knit for a 7-year-old girl.
Sample measurements:
Chest (closed): 26" (66cm)
Length: 13" (33cm)

FIT

Standard

YARN

2 skeins of Blue Sky Alpacas Dyed Cotton (100% organic cotton, 150yds [137m] per 100g skein)
      color 631 Circus Peanut (A)
1 skein of Blue Sky Alpacas Dyed Cotton (100% organic cotton, 150yds [137m] per 100g skein)
      color 618 Orchid (B)

Note: The yarn left over from the cami (see page 116) should be enough to make this matching shrug.

NEEDLES

24" (60cm) size US 10 (6mm) circular needle
size US 10 (6mm) DPNs

NOTIONS

stitch markers
stitch holders
tapestry needle

GAUGE

12 sts and 18 rows = 4" (10cm) in St st

NOTES

yo (yarn over): Wrap the working yarn around the needle and knit the next st as usual. This operation creates an eyelet hole in the knitting and inc 1 st.

pm (place marker): Slip a premade marker or a loosely knotted piece of scrap yarn in a contrasting color onto the right needle after the st just knit to mark a spot in the knitting to refer to on future rows. When you come to a marker, simply slip it from the right-hand needle to the left-hand needle.

M1 (make 1): Inc 1 st by picking up the bar between the next st and the st just knit and knitting into it.

Sl marker or sl st(s) (slip marker or slip stitch[es]): Sl a st or sts purlwise from the left needle to the right needle. When slipping a marker, knit the sts before and after it as usual.

KFB (knit 1 front and back): Inc 1 st by knitting into the front and back of the next st, creating 2 new sts on right-hand needle.

k2tog (knit 2 together): Dec 1 st by knitting 2 sts tog.

YOKE

With color B and circular needle, CO enough sts to fit loosely around the neck. Round the number of cast-on sts to the nearest even number. The sample starts with 54 sts.

Eyelet Neck Edge

ROW 1 (WS): Knit.

ROW 2 (RS): K4, *yo, k2tog; rep from * to last 4 sts, k4.

Raglan Shaping

SET-UP ROW (WS): Knit ⅓ of sts, pm for front sts; knit half of the next ⅓ of sts, pm for left sleeve; knit ⅓ of sts, pm for back; knit rem sleeve sts, place unique marker for beg of rnd.

ROW 4 (RS): K4, M1, *knit to 1 st before marker, KFB, sl marker, KFB; rep from * 3 times more, knit to last 4 sts, M1, k4—10 sts inc.

ROW 5 (WS): P4, knit to last 4 sts, p4.

Rep Rows 4–5 until the number of sts in the back section equals half the number of sts needed for desired chest measurement.

BODY

Separate Body and Sleeves

Change to color A. As you work the next row, remove the markers as you come to them.

NEXT ROW (RS): Knit across left front sts to marker, place left sleeve sts on holder, knit across back sts to marker, place right sleeve sts on another holder, knit across right front sts to end—now only the body sts are on the needle.

Work even in St st on these sts until shrug measures desired length less 1" (3cm) for edging. End with a WS row.

EYELET EDGING (RS): K4, *yo, k2tog; rep from * to last 3 or 4 sts, knit to end.

Knit 2 rows. BO knitwise on WS.

SLEEVES

Place the held sts of 1 sleeve on DPNs and join for working in the rnd. Work even in St st to desired length less 1" (3cm) for ribbing.

Count your sts. If you have an odd number, dec 1 by k2tog at the beg of the cuff.

CUFF

NEXT RND: *K1, p1; rep from * to end.

Rep this rnd 5 times more. BO loosely in rib.

FINISHING

Weave in the loose ends.

Loose shrugs like this one aren't an exact science. Try to cast on a number of sts that fits easily around the neck but not so many that it falls off the shoulders—then don't worry about it any further!

The entire yoke is worked in garter stitch, but we're keeping the first and last 4 sts in St st to make a nice rolled edge on each front.

Raglan sweaters follow the rule of thirds: ⅓ of your stitches are devoted to the front part of the sweater; ⅓ of your stitches are devoted to the back of the sweater; ⅓ of your stitches are for the sleeves, and you divide that number by 2. You'll place your stitch markers using this rule.
For a cast on of 54 sts, it looks like this:
P4, k5 for right front, pm; k9 for right sleeve, pm; k18 for back, pm; k9 for left sleeve, pm, k5, p4 for left front.

We're sizing this shrug using half the chest measurement only (in other words, the width of the back at chest level) because of the overlapping fronts.

From here on out you'll work in St st, in color A.

If the number of stitches you have doesn't quite work with this eyelet row, don't worry about it. Just try not to end the row with a yarn over.

Time to knit the sleeves. The sleeves are knit in the round, in Stockinette stitch with color A. The sleeves should not go past the elbow.

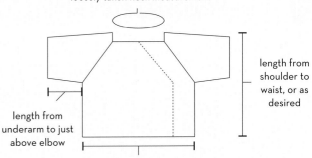

loosely taken neck measurement

length from shoulder to waist, or as desired

length from underarm to just above elbow

½ chest measurement + 1" (3cm)

Aviva

I started knitting this pattern for my daughter Ruby when she was one year old. Over the years, I've amended it to fit her as she grows, and I've since knit so many versions of it for her that I can't even remember them all. This is a pattern that you can own, changing it up as your child's body sprouts. (In fact, that's how I ended up turning this simple sweater into an even simpler dress—I just kept on going when I got to the waist [see page 124].) Use any yarn you have on hand and have some fun!

This sweater is knit in one piece, mostly in Stockinette stitch with very little sewing involved. Enjoy it!

Marcelle

FINISHED MEASUREMENTS

Measure the child's chest and add 1½–3" (4–8cm) for ease.
Sample measurements:
Chest: 33" (84cm)
Length: 20" (51cm)

FIT

Standard

YARN

2 skeins Brown Sheep Serendipity Tweed (60% cotton, 40% wool, 210yds [192m] per 113g skein)
color ST64 Cherry Blossom (MC)
1 skein Brown Sheep Serendipity Tweed (60% cotton, 40% wool, 210yds [192m] per 113g skein)
color ST68 Striped Coral Root (CC)

Note: This is a fantastic lightweight cotton-wool yarn. It feels great while you're knitting, and it sits nicely against a child's skin. The other wonderful part about this yarn is that there are 210 yards per skein, which means this yarn will go a long long way for you. I only used two skeins for Ruby. Other yarns may require more skeins.

NEEDLES

9" (23cm) size US 5 (3.75mm) Clover Plastic Mini Circular needle or set of size US 5 (3.75mm) DPNs
16" and 24" or 32" (40cm and 60cm or 80cm) size US 7 (4.5mm) circular needles

NOTIONS

4 stitch markers
2 stitch holders
tapestry needle

GAUGE

19 sts and 26 rows = 4" (10cm) in St st on larger needles

NOTES

pm (place marker): Slip a premade marker or a loosely knotted piece of scrap yarn in a contrasting color onto the right needle after the st just knit to mark a spot in the knitting to refer to on future rows. When you come to a marker, simply slip it from the right-hand needle to the left-hand needle.

Sl marker or sl st(s) (slip marker or slip stitch[es]): Slip a st or sts purlwise from the left needle to the right needle. When slipping a marker, knit the sts before and after it as usual.

KFB (knit 1 front and back): Inc 1 st by knitting into the front and back of the next st, creating 2 new sts on right-hand needle.

YOKE

With the shorter size 7 (4.5mm) circular needle and MC, CO 90 sts (as shown in sample) or enough sts to fit loosely around the neck. Pm and join for working in the rnd.

RND 1: *K1, p1; rep from * to end.

RND 2: Knit.

Rep Rnds 1–2 for approx 2" (5cm).

Raglan Increases

SET-UP ROW: Knit, pm for raglan inc as foll: Knit ⅓ of total sts, pm for front; knit ½ of next third of sts, pm for first sleeve; knit ⅓ of total sts, pm for back; knit rem sts of second sleeve, pm. If you have 90 sts, it works out like this: K30 for front, pm, k15 for left sleeve, pm, k30 for back, pm, k15 for right sleeve.

On the next rnd, start inc as foll: *KFB, knit to 1 st before next marker, KFB, sl marker; rep from * to end of rnd—8 sts inc.

NEXT RND: Knit.

Inc in this way on every other rnd until you have enough sts in the back and front sections put together to fit comfortably around the chest.

Make sure the length of the raglan (the diagonal increase line) is long enough as well. Add a few more rnds if necessary.

Divide Body and Sleeves

On the next rnd, knit across the front sts to the marker. Remove the marker, and place the left sleeve sts on a holder. Remove the next marker. Knit across the back sts to the third marker, remove it and place the right sleeve sts on another holder. Leave the beg-of-rnd marker in place.

BODY

With front and back sts united on the needle, and with beg-of-rnd marker at the right underarm, knit to the desired length for the body, less approx 1" (3cm) for the bottom ribbing.

2-Color Broken Rib

RND 1: *K1 MC, p1 CC; rep from * to end.

RND 2: *K1 MC, k1 CC; rep from * to end.

Rep Rnds 1–2 until hem measures approx 1" (3cm).

BO loosely.

SLEEVES

Put the held sleeve sts on the mini circular or DPNs. Join MC and knit around for 1" (3cm), or to desired length. Finish with 5 rnds of 2-color broken rib as for body.

BO.

FINISHING

Weave in ends and seam underarms with mattress stitch (see page 32).

To figure out how many sts you should cast on, first measure your child's neck and add 1½"–2" (4cm–5cm) of ease to that measurement. Then divide the neck measurement by 4 and multiply the product by the number of sts over 4" (10cm), referring to your gauge swatch for this number. The product of the neck measurement divided by 4 and multiplied by the number of sts over 4" (10cm) gives you the number of stitches you should cast on for the neck. If you don't come up with an even number, add a few sts to make the number even.

I wanted a loose-fitting neck that wouldn't roll down, so I knit this in broken rib.

Now you will begin increasing to create the front, back and sleeves.

The mathematical principle:
The basic idea is to think in thirds: ⅓ of your stitches are devoted to the front part of the sweater; ⅓ of your stitches are devoted to the back; ⅓ of your stitches are for the sleeves, and you divide that number by 2.

  So, for instance, if you were creating your sweater for a 6-month-old baby, your pattern would have you cast on 60 stitches. You'd knit 20, place a stitch marker, knit 10, place a stitch marker, knit 20, place a stitch marker, knit 10, place a stitch marker that's unique to mark the beg of the round, and then join. This creates the foundation for the basic raglan sweater.

To get the raglan length, measure your child from the neck to the underarm with a measuring tape.

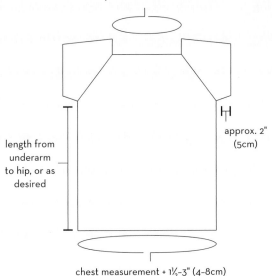

loosely taken neck measurement

length from underarm to hip, or as desired

approx. 2" (5cm)

chest measurement + 1½–3" (4–8cm)

Your cast on should be an even number of sts to accommodate the broken rib pattern. I used a needle 2 sizes smaller for the sleeves for a close-fitting cuff.

Aviva Redux:
The Dress

The dress was an accidental design; I'd been knitting the Aviva top but made the bodice too long. When I held it against the then-baby sized Ruby, I realized I'd stumbled upon an awesome idea—I'd turn my over-knitting into a dress. I'm sure many knitters have had this idea before but for me it was as INXS would say "a new sensation" to make this (maybe) naïve discovery. In any case, many dresses for Ruby later, when I sit down to knit a dress, I do so with grand intention.

Marcelle

FINISHED MEASUREMENTS
Measure the child's chest and add 1½–3" (4–8cm) for ease.
Sample measurements:
Chest: 32" (82cm)
Length from shoulder: 28" (71cm)

FIT
Standard

YARN
10 skeins Crystal Palace Bamboozle (55% bamboo, 24% cotton, 21% nylon, 90 yds [82m] per 50 g skein)
color #0435 Blueberry-Grape

NEEDLES
16" and 32" (40cm and 80cm) US 8 (5mm) circular needles
US 8 (5mm) double-pointed needles

NOTIONS
stitch markers
removable markers
stitch holders
tapestry needle

GAUGE
20 sts and 26 rows = 4" (10cm) in St st on larger needles

NOTES
pm (place marker): Slip a premade marker or a loosely knotted piece of scrap yarn in a contrasting color onto the right needle after the st just knit to mark a spot in the knitting to refer to on future rows. When you come to a marker, simply slip it from the right-hand needle to the left-hand needle.

Sl marker or sl st(s) (slip marker or slip stitch[es]): Slip a st or sts purlwise from the left needle to the right needle. When slipping a marker, knit the sts before and after it as usual.

k2tog (knit 2 together): Dec 1 st by knitting 2 sts tog.

yo (yarn over): Wrap the working yarn around the needle and knit the next st as usual. This operation creates an eyelet hole in the knitting and inc 1 st.

KFB (knit 1 front and back): Inc 1 st by knitting into the front and back of the next st, creating 2 new sts on right-hand needle.

M1 (make 1): Inc 1 st by picking up the bar between the next st and the st just knit and knitting into it.

M1P (make 1 purlwise): Inc 1 st by picking up the bar between the next st and the st just worked from back to front with the right-hand needle and purl into it.

COLLAR

With shorter circular needle, CO enough sts to fit closely around neck (sample starts with 72 sts). Do not join. Work 4 rows in St st, ending with a WS (purl) row.

EYELET ROW (RS): *K2tog, yo; rep from * to end.

Work 4 rows St st, ending with a WS row.

Fold hem to WS at the yarn over perforations. Pick up 1 st from outside of cast-on edge and k2tog—your second st is already on the left-hand needle. The key is to line these sts up.

After the picot row, work 4 rows in St st, ending with a RS row.

YOKE

Now use the rule of 3 to pm for raglan shaping: ⅓ back, ⅓ front, ⅓ divided in half for sleeves. For this design, you'll need to massage the numbers a little: Each sleeve needs an odd number of sts to center the ribbed insets and the front is worked in 2 pieces to form the V-opening, each of which needs to have the same number of sts. For our cast on of 72 sts, place the markers like this: P12 (right front), pm, p11 (right sleeve), pm, p26 (back), pm, p11 (left sleeve), pm, p12 (left front)—72 sts.

Raglan Increases and Ribbed Sleeve Insets

Find the center st of each sleeve and place a removable marker.

INC ROW (RS): Sl 1, *knit to 1 st before marker, KFB, sl marker, KFB, knit to 2 sts before marked st, p2, k1 (marked st), p2, knit to 1 st before marker, KFB, sl marker, KFB; rep from * once more, knit to last st, M1, k1—9 sts inc.

NEXT ROW (WS): Sl 1, *purl to 2 sts before marked st, k2, p1 (marked st), k2; rep from * once more, purl to last st, M1P, p1—1 st inc.

Rep the last 2 rows 4 times more.

NEXT ROW (RS): Join for working in the rnd as foll: *Knit to 1 st before marker, KFB, sl marker, KFB, knit to 2 sts before marked st, p2, k1 (marked st), p2, knit to 1 st before marker, KFB, sl marker, KFB; rep from * once more, knit to last st, pm for beg of rnd, k1—8 st inc. Do not turn. Cast on 1 st and join for working in the rnd.

NEXT RND: *Knit to 2 sts before marked st, p2, k1 (marked st), p2; rep from * once more, knit to end.

INC RND: K3, p2, *knit to 1 st before marker, KFB, sl marker, KFB, knit to 2 sts before marked st, p2, k1 (marked st), p2, knit to 1 st before marker, KFB, sl marker, KFB; rep from * once more, knit to last 2 sts, p2—8 sts inc.

NEXT RND: K3, p2, *knit to 2 sts before marked st, p2, k1 (marked st), p2; rep from * once more, knit to last 2 sts, p2.

Rep last 2 rnds to desired length, switching to larger needles as needed.

BODY

Remove all markers except beg-of-rnd marker at center front on next rnd.

NEXT RND: Work in patt across first half of front to raglan marker. Place all sleeve sts on a holder. CO 1 st. Rep for second sleeve. Knit to end of rnd. Place removable markers in each cast-on st at underarms.

Est side rib insets as foll: *Work in patt to 3 sts before marked st, p2, k3, p2; rep from * once more, work in patt to end. Cont in patt until desired starting point for bottom ruffle.

Ruffled Edge

Adjust st count, if necessary, to get a multiple of 5 sts. For example, if you have 162 body sts, dec 2 over the next rnd to 160 sts. Work in k3, p2 rib for 3 rnds, moving the beg-of-rnd marker 2 sts to the right so the rnd begins wtih p2, k3. If desired, add a ruffle to the bottom of the dress by increasing at regular intervals; for a rufflier ruffle, add many increases. For a subtle ruffle, only add a few. BO very loosely.

SLEEVES

Transfer 1 set of sleeve sts from holder to DPNs. Pick up and knit 1 st from the underarm, where you cast on 1 for the body. Knit 10 rnds, or to desired length. Remember to keep that ribbed inset in patt.

Picot Edge

EYELET RND: *K2tog, yo; rep from * to end.

Work 4 rnds even. BO.

Turn the hem to the inside of the sleeve, folding it on the eyelet line. Grab your tapestry needle and slip stitch the hem in place. When you sew a slip stitch hem, you don't stick the needle all the way through the fabric of the sleeve, lest you show your sewing skills to the whole world. Instead, pick up just a few threads of the WS of the fabric on your needle.

FINISHING

Weave in ends. Block as desired.

close neck measurement

length from under-arm to knee

approx. 1" (3cm)

5½" (14 cm)

chest measurement + 1½–3" (4–8cm)

Okay, Okay, Him Too

Patterns for Men

Knitting for men is
a double-edged sword:

They're larger, so the projects take longer, but when
you give the finished project to your Male, the look on
his face is priceless. *For me?!?! Really?* We've knit for
men of all sorts, including husbands, brothers and
friends; without fail there is always extra appreciation.
In this chapter, we have three very distinct projects
with three very distinct styles—all reflections of
the personalities of the men for whom the
projects were made.

Kendrick

My friend Kendrick wanted a brightly colored, oversized, lightweight top for casual wear, but he wanted it to have a raw, unfinished look. This was music to my ears—no weaving in those ends! He also wanted a top that would stand out, like the Big Suit David Byrne wore in the Talking Heads' live concert movie, *Stop Making Sense*—something larger than life.

As Kendrick is broad shouldered and towers over most people, I knew I would need extra yarn for his sweater. The too-long sleeves, stretched-out torso and extra-wide neck all entered into my calculations. Getting these numbers right was definitely key in the success of this sweater.

Obviously, if you want to create a boat-neck sweater for a man but don't want the raw look of the *Kendrick*, feel free to weave in the bits or add a single crochet edging around the hems. Remember: This is simply a diving board. What you bring to the project is what makes it yours.

Marcelle

FINISHED MEASUREMENTS
Chest: 60" (152cm)
Length: 29" (74cm)

FIT
Oversized (one size fits most)

YARN
3 skeins Lion Brand Micro Spun (100% microfiber acrylic, 168yds [158m] per 70g skein)
    color Lime
2 skeins Lion Brand Micro Spun in each of the following colors
    color Blue
    color Orange
    color Red
1 skein Lion Brand Micro Spun in each of the following colors
    color Fuchsia
    color Yellow
    color Coral

NEEDLES
16" and 40" (40cm and 100cm) size US 7 (4.5mm) circular needles

NOTIONS
stitch marker
tapestry needle

GAUGE
20 sts and 25 rows = 4" (10cm) in St st

NOTES

M1 (make 1): Inc 1 st by picking up the bar between the next st and the st just knit and knitting into it.

pm (place marker): Slip a premade marker or a loosely knotted piece of scrap yarn in a contrasting color onto the right needle after the st just knit to mark a spot in the knitting to refer to on future rows. When you come to a marker, simply slip it from the right-hand needle to the left-hand needle.

Sl marker or sl st(s) (slip marker or slip stitch[es]): Slip a st or sts purlwise from the left needle to the right needle. When slipping a marker, knit the sts before and after it as usual.

BACK

With lime and longer circular needle, CO 150 sts. Work 3 rows in k1, p1 rib.

Working in St st and starting with a knit row (RS), work thick and thin stripes, working the thickest stripes in lime and blue, and making the thinnest stripes in orange, fuchsia and yellow.

Cont until piece measures approx 29" (74cm) from cast-on edge.

BO with lime.

FRONT

Work the front the same as the back until it measures approx 27" (69cm) from cast-on edge.

Neck Shaping

Work 11 rows orange, ending with a WS row.

Next Row: With orange, k60, BO center 30 sts, k60.

Right Shoulder

Next Row (WS): With blue, purl.

Next Row: With blue, BO 4 sts, knit to end—56 sts.

Next Row: With yellow, purl.

Next Row: With yellow, BO 2 sts, knit to end—54 sts.

Rep last 2 rows 6 times more—42 sts.

Work 2 rows even with fuchsia.

Work 1 row even with lime.

BO with lime.

Left Shoulder

Join yarn with WS facing.

Next Row (WS): With blue, BO 4, purl to end—56 sts.

If you aren't comfortable winging it with your stripes, you can make yours exactly like the sample shown. Here are the row counts:

12 rows lime, 4 rows orange, 10 rows blue,
2 rows yellow, 6 rows fuchsia, 15 rows lime,
2 rows red, 4 rows orange, 10 rows blue,
6 rows fuchsia, 2 rows coral, 15 rows lime,
4 rows orange, 10 rows blue, 2 rows yellow,
6 rows fuchsia, 15 rows lime, 2 rows red, 4 rows orange,
10 rows blue, 6 rows fuchsia, 15 rows lime,
5 rows red, 12 rows orange, 2 rows blue,
14 rows yellow, 2 rows fuchsia, 1 row lime

NEXT ROW: With blue, knit.

NEXT ROW: With yellow, BO 2, purl to end—54 sts.

NEXT ROW: With yellow, knit.

Rep last 2 rows 6 times more—42 sts.

Work 2 rows even with fuchsia.

Work 1 row even with lime.

BO with lime.

SLEEVES (MAKE 2)

This sleeve measures 12" (31cm) in circumference at the cuff and employs a gradual increase, so that we're at 22" (56cm) by the time we get to the top.

With shorter circular needle, CO 58 sts in lime. Pm and join for working in the rnd. Work 3 rows in k1, p1 rib. Working in St st and starting with an RS row, work thick and thin stripes, working the thickest stripes in lime and blue, and making the thinnest stripes in orange, fuchsia and yellow. AT THE SAME TIME, inc 1 st at beg and end of every 7th rnd, 25 times—110 sts.

Cont until the sleeve measures approx 30" (76cm) from the cast-on row.

BO with lime.

FINISHING

You are looking at 4 pieces with lots of loose strings. You will sew the shoulders tog first. Then sew back and front tog at side seams, working from the ribbing up, leaving the top 11" (28cm) open for armholes.

Fold the sleeve flat with the increases running along the underarm. Mark the fold line with a pin and align it with the shoulder seam. Align the underarm increase line to the body side seam.

Sew sleeves into armholes, and you're done!

Well, we're back to measuring. Kendrick is muscular, so I knew I'd have to accommodate for extra girth at the top part of his arm. But he also wanted the bottom of the sleeve to be snug. Make sure to measure the man for whom you're knitting to see if you need to adjust the sweater to fit him.

The sleeves are worked from cuff to top, in the round. Read all of the sleeve instructions before starting to knit. You'll be working stripes and increasing at the same time.

The stripes as shown in the sample are worked as follows:

*12 rnds lime, 4 rnds blue, 10 rnds orange,
2 rnds fuchsia, 6 rnds yellow, 15 rnds lime,
2 rnds red, 4 rnds blue, 10 rnds orange,
6 rnds yellow, 2 rnds fuchsia, 15 rnds lime,
4 rnds blue, 10 rnds orange, 2 rnds red, 6 rnds yellow,
15 rnds lime, 10 rnds red, 4 rnds yellow,
1 rnd blue, 15 rnds orange, 1 rnd blue,
4 rnds yellow, 11 rnds red, 14 rnds lime*

Remember, this jumper has an unfinished rawness to it. Don't worry about loose ends. Unless, of course, you don't want the raw edges. In that case, you'll need to pay mind to finishing techniques such as sewing the loose strands in and out of the fabric.

Leave your tails long! For the dangling effect! Leave your tails long!

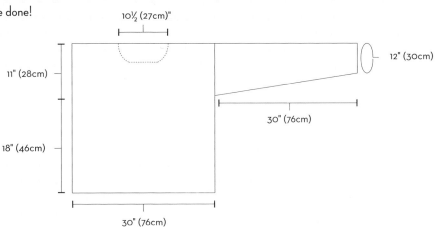

Your Boyfriend's Jumper

There's an old knitter's tale that says you mustn't knit for your boyfriend unless you want to jinx the relationship, but that after you get the ring, you can knit to your heart's content. The Knitchicks don't believe in such rubbish! Your boyfriend's jumpers are always more comfy than your own...why is that? This design by Loba van Heugten is no different. So go ahead, make it for him and then wear it yourself!

This sweater is worked in the round from the bottom up. The body and sleeves are knitted separately to the underarm, then joined on one circular needle and worked with raglan decreases up to the neck.

Pauline

FINISHED MEASUREMENTS
Chest: 42 (47, 50, 55)" (107 [120, 127, 140]cm)
Length: 24 (25½, 26½, 28)" (61 [65, 67, 71]cm)

FIT
Standard

YARN
4 (5, 5, 6) skeins Brown Sheep Lamb's Pride Bulky (85% wool, 15% mohair, 125yds [114m] per 113g skein) in each of the following colors:
color M10 Creme (A)
color M03 Grey Heather (B)

NEEDLES
32" (80cm) size US 10½ (6.5mm) circular needle
16" and 32" (40cm and 80cm) size US 11 (8mm) circular needles
size US 11 (8mm) DPNs
size US 10½ (6.5mm) DPNs

NOTIONS
stitch markers
removable markers
stitch holders
tapestry needle

GAUGE
10 sts and 32 rows = 4" (10cm) in 2-color brioche st with larger needles

NOTES

yo (yarn over): Wrap the working yarn around the needle and knit the next st as usual. This operation creates an eyelet hole in the knitting and inc 1 st.

brk (brioche knit stitch): Knit the yo tog with the slipped st from the previous rnd.

LLI (Left lifted increase): Inc 1 st by inserting the tip of the right needle into the back of the st 1 row below on the left needle and purling into it to create a left-leaning increase.

RLI (right lifted increase): Inc 1 st by inserting the tip of the right needle into the back of the st 1 row below on the left needle and knitting into it to create a right-leaning increase.

M1 (make 1): Inc 1 st by picking up the bar between the next st and the st just knit and knitting into it.

brp (brioche purl stitch): Purl the yo tog with the slipped st from the previous rnd.

SSK (slip, slip, knit): Dec 1 st by slipping 2 sts knitwise 1 at a time, inserting the tip of the left needle into both sts and knitting the 2 sts tog.

k2tog (knit 2 together): Dec 1 st by knitting 2 sts tog.

Sl marker or sl st(s) (slip marker or slip stitch[es]): Slip a st or sts purlwise from the left needle to the right needle. When slipping a marker, knit the sts before and after it as usual.

2-COLOR BRIOCHE STITCH (MULTIPLE OF 2 STS)

Sl all sts purlwise with yarn in back.

RND 1: With B, *yo, sl 1, brp; rep from * to end.

RND 2: With A, *brk, yo, sl 1; rep from * to end.

Rep Rnds 1–2 for patt.

BODY

With color B and smaller circular needle, CO 104 (116, 124, 136) sts. Join for working in the rnd. Place a removable marker in the first st and the 53rd (59th, 63rd, 69th) st.

SET-UP RND: With A, *k1, yo, sl 1; rep from * to end.

Begin working 2-Color Brioche Stitch. Work even for 2" (5cm), then change to larger circular needle. Work even until body measures 13 (13½, 14, 14½)" (33 [34, 36, 37]cm) from cast-on edge, ending with Rnd 1 of patt.

Underarm Gusset Shaping

RND 1: With A, brk (marked st), LLI, *yo, sl 1, brk; rep from * to 1 st before marked st, yo, sl 1, RLI, brk (marked st), LLI, *yo, sl 1, brk; rep from * to 1 st before marked st, yo, sl 1, RLI—4 sts inc.

RND 2: With B, [M1, yo, sl 1] twice, *brp, yo, sl 1; rep from * to marked st, [M1, yo, sl 1] twice, *brp, yo, sl 1; rep from * to end—4 sts inc.

RND 3: With A, yo, sl 1, *brk, yo, sl 1; rep from * to last st, brk.

RND 4: With B, *brp, yo, sl 1; rep from * to end.

RNDS 5–6: Rep Rnds 3–4.

Notes on Brioche Stitch:
Because of the use of slipped stitches, each visible "row" in two-color brioche stitch is actually two rows (one row with color A and one row with color B).

When counting stitches or working decreases, treat each slipped stitch and its accompanying yarn over as a single stitch.

RND 7: With A, [yo, sl 1, brk] twice, LLI, *yo, sl 1, brk; rep from * to 3 sts before marked st, yo, sl 1, RLI, [brk, yo, sl 1] twice, brk, LLI, *yo, sl 1, brk; rep from * to last st, RLI, brk—4 sts inc.

RND 8: With B, [brp, yo, sl 1] twice, M1, *yo, sl 1, brp; rep from * to 3 sts before marked st, yo, sl 1, M1, yo, sl 1, [brp, yo, sl 1] twice, M1, *yo, sl 1, brp; rep from * to last 2 sts, yo, sl 1, M1, yo, sl 1—4 sts inc; 120 (132, 140, 152) sts.

RNDS 9–24: Rep Rnds 3–4 8 times. End last rnd 3 sts before marked st.

At each side of the body you will have 7 sts in a branching patt formed by the inc, beg and ending with sts in color B, with the marked st in color A in the center. Place these 7 sts on holders for underarms. Do not cut yarn—53 (59, 63, 69) sts rem for back and front.

Set body aside while you work sleeves.

SLEEVES (MAKE 2)

With smaller DPNs and color B, CO 24 (26, 28, 32) sts. Place a removable marker in first st.

SET-UP RND: *K1, yo, sl 1; rep from * to end.

Begin working 2-Color Brioche Stitch. Work even until sleeve measures 4" (10cm) from cast-on edge, ending with Rnd 1.

Change to larger needles and begin inc.

RND 1: With A, brk (marked st), LLI, yo, sl 1, *brk, yo, sl 1; rep from * to end, RLI—2 sts inc.

RND 2: With B, [yo, sl 1] twice, *brp, yo, sl 1; rep from * to end.

RND 3: With A, brk, *brk, yo, sl 1; rep from * to last st, brk.

RNDS 4–9: Rep Rnds 2–3 3 times.

RND 10: With B, yo, sl 1, M1, *yo, sl 1, brp; rep from * to last st, yo, sl 1, M1—2 sts inc'd.

RND 11: With A, *brk, yo, sl 1; rep from * to end.

RND 12: With B, *yo, sl 1, brp; rep from * to end.

RNDS 13–22: Rep Rnds 7–8 5 times.

At end of Rnd 22, shift sts so that marked st is the first st on the first DPN.

Rep Rnds 1–22 3 times more—40 (42, 44, 46) sts. Change to 16" (40cm) circular needle when necessary.

Work even until sleeve measures 18 (18½, 19, 19)" (46 [47, 48, 48]cm), or desired length to underarm, ending with a rnd in color B. End last rnd 3 sts before marked st.

As you did on the body, put 7 underarm sts on a holder (marked st is in center of this group)—33 (35, 37, 39) sts rem.

Cut yarn, leaving a long tail to use in seaming underarms later. Set aside and work second sleeve.

YOKE

Unite all sts of body and sleeves on larger circular needle as foll: With A and circular needle holding body sts, work in est patt across sts of one sleeve, pm. Work across body sts to held underarm sts, pm. Work across sts of second sleeve, pm. Work across body sts to end of rnd, pm—172 (188, 200, 216) sts.

Raglan Shaping

RND 1: With B, work even in est patt.

RND 2: With A, *SSK, work in est patt to 2 sts before marker, k2tog, sl marker; rep from * 3 times more—8 sts dec.

RND 3: With B, work even in est patt.

RND 4: With A, work even in est patt.

Rep Rnds 1–4 until 44 (44, 48, 48) sts rem.

TURTLENECK

Change to 16" (40 cm) circular needle if necessary. Work even in est patt until neck measures 9" (23cm), ending with a rnd in color A.

BO loosely with color B.

FINISHING

Join underarm seams using three needle bind off.

Weave in ends.

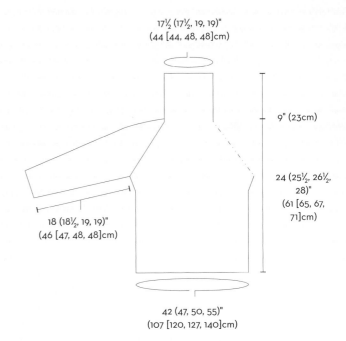

17½ (17½, 19, 19)"
(44 [44, 48, 48]cm)

9" (23cm)

24 (25½, 26½, 28)"
(61 [65, 67, 71]cm)

18 (18½, 19, 19)"
(46 [47, 48, 48]cm)

42 (47, 50, 55)"
(107 [120, 127, 140]cm)

Michael

Maren Waxenberg, craftswoman extraordinaire, designed this sweater for her husband, Michael, using his favorite colors. She wanted to create something that looked difficult to knit, but the *Michael* is in fact effortless. This pattern has you working the body as a tube with minimal shaping, then sewing the sleeves on later. Oh, yes, darling Knitchick, the *Michael* employs the Norwegian Steeking Technique (see pages 106–107). Don't blanch. We're going to get you to cut through your knitting as if you were cutting through a piece of cloth.

Marcelle

FINISHED MEASUREMENTS

Measure the man's chest and add 4" (10cm) for ease.
For example, the sample as shown was knit for a size Large man.
Sample measurements:
Chest: 48" (122cm)
Length: 25½" (65cm)

FIT

Standard to Loose

YARN

4 skeins Brown Sheep Top of the Lamb Worsted (100% wool, 190yds [174m] per 113g skein)
   color 310 Peacock (MC)
3 skeins Brown Sheep Top of the Lamb Worsted (100% wool, 190yds [174m] per 113g skein)
   color 331 Mallard (CC)

NEEDLES

16" and 32" (40cm and 80cm) size US 8 (5mm) circular needles
size US 6 (4mm) DPNs

NOTIONS

stitch marker
1 package polyester hem tape in matching color
sewing needle and thread
tapestry needle

GAUGE

20 sts and 28 rows = 4" (10cm) in St st

NOTES

SSK (slip, slip, knit): Dec 1 st by slipping 2 sts knitwise 1 at a time, inserting the tip of the left needle into both sts and knitting the 2 sts tog.

k2tog (knit 2 together): Dec 1 st by knitting 2 sts tog.

pm (place marker): Slip a premade marker or a loosely knotted piece of scrap yarn in a contrasting color onto the right needle after the st just knit to mark a spot in the knitting to refer to on future rows. When you come to a marker, simply slip it from the right-hand needle to the left-hand needle.

BODY

With larger circular needle and CC, CO the number of sts needed for desired chest size. Pm and join for working in the rnd. For the sample, we cast on 240 sts.

RND 1: *K5, p5; rep from * to end.

Rep Rnd 1 for 2½" (6cm).

To work the moss st patterning on the rest of the body, you'll need a multiple of 4 sts. If necessary, inc or dec a few sts evenly spaced over the next rnd (first rnd of the piping) to get the right number of sts.

The gansey shown here uses a k5, p5 rib on the bottom edge, so you'll need a multiple of 10 sts. Or, if that doesn't work for the size you want, you can substitute another rib pattern such as k2, p2 (multiple of 4 stitches) or the very traditional k1, p1 (multiple of 2 stitches).

Piping Rows

Work in the piping patt as foll:

Purl 2 rnds with CC.

Knit 2 rnds with MC.

Knit 1 rnd with CC.

Purl 2 rnds with CC.

The piping consists of the horizontal bars that section off the moss stitch bits. It's a very nice decorative look against the sea of moss.
Be sure to check where your colors are landing as you're trying to checkerboard the blue/green.

Moss Stitch

Work in moss st as foll:

RND 1: *K2 CC, k2 MC; rep from * to end.

RND 2: With MC, *p2, k2; rep from * to end.

RND 3: *K2 MC, k2 CC: rep from * to end.

RND 4: With MC, *k2, p2; rep from * to end.

Rep Rnds 1–4 once more, then Rnds 1–2 again for a total of 10 rnds moss st.

Knit 1 rnd with MC.

Knit 1 rnd with CC.

Now go back to the beg. Not the cast on or the ribbing, but the piping.

Work the 7 piping rnds, then the 10 moss st rnds foll by 2 St st rnds. Keep alternating until you've reached the desired body length. End with 7 piping rnds.

Measure the length from the neck to just where his hip bone juts out.

Finish neck edge by working 6 rnds in St st with MC. This edge will fold over to become the neckline facing.

SLEEVES (MAKE 2)

With shorter circular needle and CC, CO the number of sts needed for top of sleeve. Pm and join for working in the rnd. For the sample sleeve, we cast on 100 sts.

Knit 6 rnds to create a facing that will be tacked to the inside of the sweater, just like at the neckline.

Piping Rows

Purl 2 rnds with CC.

Knit 2 rnds with MC.

Knit 1 rnd with CC.

Purl 2 rnds with CC.

Knit 1 rnd with CC.

Knit 11 rows of blue, then 1 rnd with CC.

Alternate the piping and St st sections until the sleeve measures approx 8" (20cm) from the last rnd of the facing.

Shaping

NEXT RND: K1, k2tog, knit to last 3 sts, SSK, k1—2 sts dec.

Dec as est on every 4th rnd, maintaining the patt, until you reach desired sleeve length less 2½" (6cm). End after working a piping section.

CUFF

Change to DPNs.

RND 1: *K5, p5; rep from * to end.

Rep Rnd 1 for 2½" (6cm).

BO loosely.

Attach the sleeves using the Norwegian Steeking technique (see pages 106–107).

FINISHING

Seam shoulders for 5" (13cm) on each side.

Use sewing needle and thread to attach hem tape to WS of neckline. Fold facing down over WS and slip stitch in place using yarn threaded on a tapestry needle.

Weave in ends.

The sleeves are worked from the top down to the cuff. The pattern is piping in CC alternating with St st in MC.

How do you calculate the number of sts for the top of the sleeve? Take the armhole depth of the person you're knitting for and add ½"–1" (1cm–3cm) for ease. Multiply this number by 2, then multiply the result by your gauge (5 stitches per inch or 2 stitches per centimeter). Round to the nearest even number.

The armhole depth is taken by measuring in a straight line from the top of the shoulder to the underarm. For most men, this will be around 9"–10" (23cm–25cm). For teenage boys it may be as short as 8" (20cm).

The sleeve length of the sample is about 21" (53cm).

The cuff is worked in the same k5, p5 rib used on the body, so again you'll need a multiple of 10 stitches. You can skip the last few decreases if needed, and simply work even to the desired length, or you can decrease a few extra stitches on the last piping round to get to a multiple of 10.

Why such a small-sized needle? For the dramatic cuff effect!

You don't necessarily have to use DPNs. You can try one of those super-mini circulars that do the trick just as well.

The hem tape on the neckline functions as a stabilizer. The woven tape prevents the knitted neckline from stretching out.

armhole depth +½–1"
(1–3cm)

length from shoulder to
hip bone, or as desired

length from underarm
to wrist

chest measurement + 4" (10cm)

Abbreviations
STANDARD KNITTING ABBREVIATIONS

beg	begin, beginning
CC	contrast color
dec	decrease, decreased, decreasing
dpn(s)	double-pointed needle(s)
foll	following
inc	increase, increased, increasing
k	knit
KFB	knit 1 front and back
k2tog	knit 2 together
k3tog	knit 3 together
LLI	left lifted increase
M1	make one
M1L	make one left
M1R	make one right
MC	main color
p	purl
(in) patt	(in pattern)
pm	place marker
psso	pass slipped stitch over
p2tog	purl 2 together
p3tog	purl 3 together
rem	remaining
rep	repeat
RLI	right lifted increase
rnd	round
RS	right side
SKP	slip 1, knit 1, pass slipped stitch over
SK2P	slip 1, knit 2 together, pass slipped stitch over
sl	slip
SSK	slip, slip, knit
st(s)	stitch(es)
St st	Stockinette stitch
work 2 tog	work 2 together
WS	wrong side
yf	yarn forward
yo	yarn over

Resources

Many of the yarns and supplies used to make the projects in this book can be found in your local yarn store. If you have trouble finding exactly what you want, use the manufacturer information provided here to find online and local vendors.

GEAR

Lantern Moon
www.lanternmoon.com
(800) 530-4170
handcrafted knitting and crochet supplies, including bags, baskets, notions, needles and silk yarn

Lexie Barnes Bags and Accessories
www.lexiebarnes.com
(413) 303-1440
all kinds of bags, totes and pouches

Lisa G
www.lisag.com.au
handmade needles, knitting bags and needle rolls

Namaste Inc
www.namasteneedles.com
(818) 717-9134
handbags, totes, pouches and notions cases for knitting and beyond

Further Reading

YARN

Blue Sky Alpacas
www.blueskyalpacas.com
(888) 460-8862

Brown Sheep
www.brownsheep.com
(800) 826-9136

Cascade Yarns
www.cascadeyarns.com

**Crystal Palace Yarns/Straw
Into Gold, Inc.**
www.crystalpalaceyarns.com
www.straw.com

Karabella Yarns
www.karabellayarns.com

Knitting Fever
www.knittingfever.com
(516) 546-3600

Lion Brand Yarns
www.lionbrand.com

Lorna's Laces
www.lornaslaces.net

Muench Yarns
www.muenchyarns.com
(800) 733-9276

Isager
www.isagerknit.com

Rowan
www.knitrowan.com

Misti Alpaca
www.mistialpaca.com
(888) 776-9276

Lang Yarns
www.langyarns.ch/en/

Manos Del Uruguay
http://manosdeluruguay.co.uk

Westminster Fibers
www.westminsterfibers.com
(800) 445-9276

BOOKS

Knitting from the Top
by Barbara G. Walker

**The Knitting Answer Book: Solutions to Every
Problem You'll Ever Face; Answers to Every Question
You'll Ever Ask**
by Margaret Radcliffe

WEB SITES

Craft Yarn Council of America
http://craftyarncouncil.com

Knitchicks
www.knitchicks.co.uk

The Knitting Guild Association
www.tkga.com

Ravelry
www.ravelry.com

Index

A

abbreviations, 140

B

backward-loop cast on, 19
binding off, 31
blocking, 38
brioche stitch, 134

C

cable cast on, 23
cables, knitting, 111
casting on
    backward-loop cast on, 19
    cable, 23
    knitting on, 22
    long-tail method, 20–21
    multiple stitches, 18
casting off, 31
chart
    Argyle, 57
    DiamondLace, 99
    Diamonds, 52
    handy dandy Knitchicks, 39
    Lace Motif, 60
    Waves, 73
circular knitting, 9, 35
circular needles, 36
construction method, 35
continental method
    knitting, 25
    purling, 27
Craft Yarn Council of America, 13
cuff, belled, 81

D

decreasing, 30
double-pointed needles, 36–38
drying yarn, 14

E

edges
    picot, 114
    raw, 129–131
embroidered embellishments, 105
ends, loose, 38

English method
    knitting, 24
    purling, 26

F

finishing, 38
fit, 34
Four Noble Tips, 36
fringe, 105

G

garter stitch hem, 45

H

history of knitting, 9

I

increasing, 28–29

J

jumper, basics of knitting, 34–38

K

k2tog (knit 2 together), 30
Kitchener stitch, 32–33
knit stitch, 24
knitting on, 22
knitting abbreviations, 140
knitting blind, 83
knitting flat, 37–38
knitting needles
    cable, 111
    circular. See circular needles
    storing, 10
    transferring from circulars to DPNS
    (or vice versa), 37
    types of, 11
knitting in the round, 35. See also Circular knitting

L

ladder, 37
long-tail method, casting on, 20–21
loose ends, 38
losing track of rows, 37

M

M1 (make one), 29
mattress stitch, 32
measuring, 45, 76
moss stitch, 138

n

necklines
  choosing, 35
  fitted neck band, 86
  roll-top cowl, 44
  ruffled, 113–115
  turtleneck, 135
  V-neck, 53, 77
  V-neck lace-up, 63–65
needle size chart, 11
needles. See knitting needles
Norwegian steeking technique, 106–107
notions, 15

P

p2tog (purl 2 together), 30
picking, 18
  knit stitch, 25
  purl stitch, 27
    See also continental method
picking up stitches, 38
picot hem, 76, 114
projects for babies
  cable (Oscar), 108–110
  diamond lace (Baby Diamond), 98–99
projects for children
  cami (Ruby's Cami), 117–119
  dress (Aviva Redux), 124–125
  embroidered (Kaia), 103–105
  ruffled neckline (Ruby Ruffle), 113–115
  shrug (Ruby's Shrug), 120–121
  short-sleeved, stockinette stitch (Aviva), 122–123
  short-sleeved, striped (Jarrah), 100–101
projects for men
  boat-neck, with raw-edges (Kendrick), 129–131
  moss stitch (Michael), 137–139
  turtleneck sweater (Boyfriend's Jumper), 133–135
projects for women
  argyle pattern (Isla), 55–57
  hourglass rib (Loba), 71–73
  neck band (Summer), 85–87
  peek-a-boo cutout (Marcelle), 59–61
  pink piping and lace insert (Raven), 79–81
  reversible long-sleeved (Moni), 89–91
  ribbed diamond pattern vest (Allez Héléne), 51–53
  roll-top sleeveless cowl (Shula), 43–45
  short-sleeve mesh pattern (Layla), 93–95
  sleeveless cowl (Jess), 47–49
  V-neck horizontal stripes (Pam), 75–77
  V-neck lace-up (Morgan/Mini Morgan), 63–65, 67–69
  wrap sweater (Thelma & Louise), 82–83
purl stitch, 26–27

R

raglan sweater, 36
resources, 140–141
rule of thirds, 64

S

scooping yarn, 25
sewing up seams, 32–33, 38
single-needle knitting, 9
sleeves
  cap, 72
  choosing, 35
  knitting flat for, 38
  short-sleeve mesh pattern, 95
  top-down, 36
slip knot, 17
SSK (slip, slip, knit), 30
stacking stitches, 76
stair-stepping, 37
Standard Yarn Weight System, 13
steeking technique, 106–107
stitches
  picking up, 38
  See also entries for specific stitches
stockinette stitch, 27
stranded colorwork technique, 56
sweater, basics of knitting, 34–38

T

tails, 17
techniques, 16–33. See also entries for specific techniques
tension, 19, 25
threads, dangling, 38
throwing, 18
  knit stitch, 24
  purl stitch, 26
  See also English method

W

washing yarn, 14
weaving in ends, 38
"work both sides at once," 31
wraps per inch (WPI) method, 14

Y

yarn
  caring for, 14
  choosing, 34
  fibers, 12
  gauge, 14
  label, 14
  resources for, 141
  types of, 12

Find More Great Knitting Patterns in These North Light Books

These books and other fine North Light books are available at your local bookstore or online supplier. Or visit our Web site, *www.mycraftivity.com.*

CLOSELY KNIT
Handmade Gifts for the Ones You Love
Hannah Fettig

Closely Knit is filled with thoughtful knitted gifts to fit all the people you love: special handknits for mothers, daughters, sisters, the men in your life, precious wee ones and treasured friends. From luxurious scarves and wearable sweaters to cozy socks and even a quick-to-knit heart pin, there really is something for everyone on your list in this book. Projects range from quick and simple to true labors of love, and each is rated with a handy time guide so you can choose what to knit based on how much time you have. Bonus quick-fix options will save the day when you need to whip up a meaningful gift in a jiffy.

ISBN-13: 978-1-60061-018-9
ISBN-10: 1-60061-018-8
paperback with flaps, 144 pages, Z1280

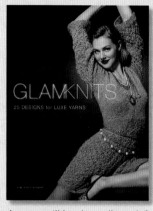

GLAM KNITS
Stefanie Japel

Glam Knits showcases 26 totally glam designs by Stefanie Japel, best-selling author of Fitted Knits. Each of the Glam Knits pieces is knit with decadent luxe yarns that are a pleasure to knit and wear. Whether you choose to knit a sinfully soft cashmere cardigan, a sparkling silk cami or an eye-catching metallic dress, you'll be the walking definition of glamour when you wear your finished creation. And don't forget to knit that special finishing touch. The Glam Knits collection is rounded out with stylish accent pieces such as a lacy scarf and even a fluffy fur collar. Every design is easily customizable for a perfect fit, and each pattern is given in sizes from extra small to extra large—plus instructions in the front of the book walk you through the ins and outs of modifying a pattern.

ISBN-13: 978-1-60061-035-6
ISBN-10: 1-60061-035-8
paperback with flaps, 144 pages, Z1378

SOFT & SIMPLE KNITS FOR LITTLE ONES
45 Easy Projects
Heidi Boyd

Soft + Simple Knits for Little Ones is packed with tons of bright and cute handknits to make for the special little ones in your life, whether you're a beginner or an expert knitter. Best of all, every design is functional and touchable, guaranteed to get plenty of use and love. From a cozy stroller blanket with clever ties and a pocket for a small stuffed bear, to a cotton rollneck sweater with an intarsia giraffe, this book has something to make any wee one happy. Even if you've never picked up a set of knitting needles, a helpful techniques section teaches you the skills needed to quickly and successfully complete each of the projects in this book without spending too much money or too much time.

ISBN-13: 978-1-58180-965-7
ISBN-10: 1-58180-965-4
paperback with flaps, 160 pages, Z0696

PINTS & PURLS
Portable Projects for the Social Knitter
Karida Collins & Libby Bruce

Pints & Purls features over 30 patterns specifically designed for social knitting, from super-simple projects including armwarmers and dishrags to more complex pieces such as socks with easy repeats and an entrelac wrap. You don't have to knit alone on your couch or on the bus—social knitting is about getting together with a group of friends to enjoy each other's company and work on a project you love. It's about being so excited about your knitting that you're not willing to leave it at home when you go out. Each pattern is rated by drink level so you know just how distracted you can be while you knit your project. And if you do mess up, there are plenty of tips and tricks for fixing your mistakes. So grab your knitting bag and your buddies, and head out on the town for some social knitting.

ISBN-13: 978-1-60061-146-9
ISBN-10: 1-60061-146-X
paperback, 160 pages, Z2387